1/15/85

RENEWING THE MIND:
The Arena For Success

To:
Dean & Gail Taylor

Because we love you, we want you to have the very best God has for you, including this book!

Love ya,
Joe & Helen

This book presents the theme and foundation of a ministry that grew from thirty to several thousand people in less than five years. Growth is a Christian way of life and the key to all spiritual growth is the Renewing of the Mind. I learned this as a drug addict searching for a new life. After being born again in 1974, I soon realized that there were many problems in my life that being saved did not solve. Like so many Christians I thought that once I was born again everything would be perfect. Thank God, I found Romans 12:2, "And be not conformed to this world but be ye transformed by the renewing of your mind that ye may prove what is that good, and acceptable, and perfect will of God."

I have attempted to present the knowledge I have gained about Renewing the Mind through study and through living the Word in a way that will inspire and help people. I know there is much to be learned from the Lord, but this is a start toward the "good, acceptable, and perfect will of God."

Casey Treat

September 1984

RENEWING THE MIND: The Arena For Success

by Casey Treat

Published by
Christian Faith Center
and
Casey Treat Ministries
P.O. Box 98581
Seattle, Washington 98188

All scripture text is taken from the King James Version unless otherwise specified with permission granted as stated below.

The New Testament: An Expanded Translation, by Kenneth S. Wuest; William B. Eerdman Publishing Company

Williams New Testament, by Charles B. Williams; Moody Press, Chicago, Il.

Verses marked TLB are taken from *The Living Bible,* copyright 1971 by Tyndale House Publishers, Wheaton, Il. Used by permission.

Scriptures taken from The Holy Bible: New International Version. Copyright 1973, 1978 by the International Bible Society. Used by permission of Zondervan Bible Publishers.

Scripture quotations from Amplified New Testament, Copyright The Lockman Foundation 1954, 1958.

Second Printing, 1985

ISBN 0-931697-01-8

Published by: Casey Treat Ministries
               P.O. Box 98581
               Seattle, Washington 98188

TABLE OF CONTENTS

Introduction

This book is dedicated to Julius Young, who introduced me to Jesus, and with whom hours of discussion have been spent on the Renewing of the Mind. Also, I greatly thank the staff and congregation at Christian Faith Center who have made this book a reality. Especially Kathy Coyer and Debbie Willis, whose hours of commitment were indispensible.

INTRODUCTION

Casey Treat is a tremendous blessing to the body of Christ with his great teaching of Biblical truths. God has gifted him with an exciting and unique way of ministering. All who are fortunate enough to see and hear him, know that God is using him mightily.

Casey is a good example of what the Lord wants to do for us, if we will surrender our lives to Him. Casey started out like many of us, lost and searching for the truth in all the wrong places. When the Lord touched his life and Casey began to renew his mind, God, through His Word, began to reveal to him the keys to success in every area of life.

God, in His infinite wisdom, has laid before us life and death, blessing and cursing, and we have the right to choose. Receive the life and the blessings God has provided for you, and enter into the arena for success by renewing your mind to God's Word.

It will change your life!

Roosevelt "Rosey" Grier

1
BORN OF THE SPIRIT

To be a Christian, and a part of God's kingdom, you must be spiritually born. You are already physically, or "fleshly" born, but to be a *Christian* you must be born again. Jesus told Nicodemus in John 3:3 & 6,

> Except a man be born again he cannot see the kingdom of God. That which is born of the flesh is flesh, but that which is born of the Spirit is spirit.

You may not realize it, but you are a spirit being. The real you is not a body, or a mind, but a spirit.

You are made in the image of God, and God is a spirit. Look in Genesis 1:26.

> Let us make man in our image, after our likeness.

And John 4:24 says,

> God is a spirit: and they that worship him must worship him in spirit and in truth.

1

It doesn't say God is a mind, or a body; it says, "God is a spirit". That means you are a spirit, because you are made in God's image.

When you are born again, the real you, or your spirit man is born. Instead of being spiritually dead, and separated from God, you now have eternal life, and fellowship with God. John 3:16-18 says,

> For God so loved the world, that he gave his only begotten Son, that whosoever believeth in him should not perish, but have everlasting life. For God sent not his Son into the world to condemn the world; but that the world through him might be saved. He that believeth on him is not condemned: but he that believeth not is condemned already, because he hath not believed in the name of the only begotten Son of God.

This takes place in the spirit, not in the soul, (or mental realm) and not in the physical realm. When you were born again, your mind, and body stayed the same, but your spirit was recreated. Paul said in II Corinthians 5:17,

> Therefore if any man be in Christ, he is a new creature: old things are passed away; behold, all things are become new.

It's obvious that all your old thoughts didn't pass away, because you still remember the same things you did before you were saved. If you thought about money problems before you were saved, you still thought about them afterwards. If you thought about getting drunk on Saturday night before you got saved, that thought came back to you afterwards. Even though the initial peace and joy of salvation affects your way of thinking, basically your head is still in the same condition. It is your spirit that has been recreated.

Your body stays the same too. If you were tall, with red hair before you got saved, you still are now. If you were 45 pounds overweight, you probably still are now. The point is, the new birth is a spiritual experience which changes the human spirit from being dead, and separated from God, to a live spirit, fellowshipping with God. As a born again believer, you are now in the family of God, and on your way to heaven. You are now the righteousness of God, and there is no condemnation on your life. (Col. 1:12, 13; II Cor. 5:21; Rom. 8:1) If we Christians could just plug into this new spirit, we could walk through life from the day we were born again overcoming every circumstance. But ... we still have a soul, and a body to deal with.

Your soul is your mind, your emotions, and your will. This is where your thinking, reasoning, and imagining takes place, and you decide how to react, or respond to the circumstances of life. Remember, your soul is not born again.

Neither is your body. Your body is your house here on earth. Peter called it a tent for your spirit man to live in.

The soul realm is where we Christians have the most trouble. It is in our thinking, or reasoning that we reject the information given by our spirit, and do our own thing. Even though our spirit is born again, and the Holy Spirit now lives in us, we very quickly overlook what He says.

The *key* to successful Christian living is to get your mind to line up with the spirit, and obey what the spirit man says. Romans 8:6,7 tells us,

> For to be carnally minded is death; but to be spiritually minded is life and peace. Because the carnal mind is enmity against God; for it is not subject to the law of God, neither indeed can be.

Notice, you can think two ways; carnally or spiritually. You have the choice to think as the flesh tells you to, or as your spirit tells you to. Carnal means 'flesh', so the carnal mind is one that thinks in line with the body, or the world. Your body might tell you to do anything at any time. Sometimes it wants to be lazy, it may want to get fat, it may even want to commit adultery. And if your head goes along with your body, you will be in trouble *all* the time. Because, your body is not yet redeemed. Romans 8:23 says,

Even we ourselves groan within ourselves, waiting for the adoption, to wit,
the redemption of our body.

Your body is in contact with the natural world,
where Satan is still lord. II Corinthians 4:4
says,

In whom the god of this age has blinded
the minds of those who do not believe,
lest the light of the gospel of the glory of
Christ, who is the image of God, should
shine on them.

The god of this world, Satan, can attack your
flesh with all kinds of negativity. But if your
mind is spiritual, and not carnal, you won't
allow Satan's attacks to influence you.
Romans 8:5,6 tells us,

For they that are after the flesh do mind
the things of the flesh; but they that are
after the Spirit the things of the spirit.
For to be carnally minded is death; but
to be spiritually minded is life and
peace.

A spiritual mind is one that thinks in line
with the Spirit of God, and the Word of God. It
has been renewed, the old ways of thinking are
swept out, and replaced with new thought patterns. Most born again believers have never
been taught how to renew their minds, and so
their carnal mind has them in a constant

dilemma. They love the Lord, and are going to heaven, but they're not enjoying their rights, and privileges as a Christian right now. If we are just supposed to get saved, and then wait till we get to heaven to receive God's riches, we wouldn't need the Holy Spirit *now*. We wouldn't need the weapons of our warfare *now*. And the Bible would only have to be one page long. You see, God wants us to receive His abundant life *right now*, but we must be *spiritually minded* to do so. The carnal mind is the enemy, or in opposition to God, but the spiritual mind is life and peace. It doesn't matter how much praying, confessing, and interceding you do; if your mind is messed up, you will not receive the things you desire. Notice Paul said, "The carnal mind is enmity against God". In Romans 8:8, Paul says,

> So then they that are in the flesh cannot please God.

The spiritual mind *always* agrees with the Word, and Spirit of God. For instance: you may have financial pressure on you right now. So you sit down to think about what you should do. Right away your spirit says, "Give and it shall be given unto you; good measure, pressed down, shaken together, and running over shall men give into your bosom" (Luke 6:38). Then you think, "If I give away more money, I'll have less to pay the bills with, and be worse off than before." Then your spirit says, "Bring ye all the tithes into the storehouse, that there may be meat in mine house, and prove me now herewith, saith the Lord of hosts, if I will not open you the windows of heaven, and pour you out a blessing, that there shall not be room enough to receive it. And I will rebuke the devourer for your sakes, and he shall not destroy the fruits of your ground." (Malachi 3:10, 11) But your head comes back with, "No way! That only works for those preachers! The every day guy like me will never receive the blessings of God." So you decide to try to borrow, and beg your way out of your problem in your own way. Do you see what happened? Your own thinking overrode your spirit, which was in agreement with the Word, and the Spirit of God. Your spirit was trying to lead you in God's way, to victory. But the carnal mind won't receive the things of God. It will reject them *every time.*

I'm sure you've been in a position where someone has made you mad, and you thought, "I'd like to give them a piece of my mind!" Then inside you heard, "Just be cool, and love this person. They don't even know what they're doing." But you went ahead, and opened your mouth anyway, and told them off good! Now they *really* know how loving, patient, and kind a Christian is.

Because of wrong thinking, we lose our control, and bring many problems on ourselves. The carnal mind will keep you in trouble while the spiritual mind is life and peace.

The mind is the fulcrum between a positive spiritual life, and a negative carnal life. The two choices are ever before you, and you must constantly exercise your will to be spiritually minded. When you are first born again, it seems the decision to be spiritually minded is very hard. Every time you turn around, there's an opportunity to see something negative, do something negative, or say something negative. Many times you dive right into it. Sometime later you come up feeling guilty, and asking the Lord why you did that. It's because your mind is not renewed to the Word of God. The more carnal thinking you are involved with, the harder it is to walk with God.

So you must use your will, and begin to change the way you think. When the Word of God comes to mind, act on it without trying to reason it out. Just do what God said, whether you understand it or not. If you try to figure out everything the spirit says, you will always be carnally minded. I know people who have been trying to figure out the Bible for years, and they still can't do it. They are just as goofy (or goofier) now, as when they started. To be spiritually minded, you must act the Word of God, and think on the Word of God, whether you understand it or not. If the Bible says, "By whose stripes ye were healed" (I Peter 2:24), then you think, "I'm healed", and act like your healed; *regardless* of whether you understand it or not. If the Bible says, "I can do all things through Christ", then think, and act like you can! If the Bible says, "Give and it shall be given unto you", then you should act on that, *no matter what.*

Ephesians 2:8-9 tells us,

> For by grace are ye saved through faith;
> and that not of yourselves: it is the gift
> of God. Not of works, lest any man
> should boast.

You can't improve the salvation of your spirit.
You cannot add to it, you cannot make it better.
You cannot do anything to the salvation of
your spirit, except receive it. It's a gift, not of
works. Unfortunately, a lot of people get confused right there, and say, "Well, I'm saved by
faith, not by works, so I'm not going to do anything. I'm not going to tithe, that's works. I'm
not going to study the Bible, that's works. I'm
not going to pray, that's works. God takes care
of all that for me. I'm saved by grace, through
faith."

True, you can't add to salvation, you can't
improve salvation, you can't make it any better; but... you still have a soul, and a body, and
they are *not* saved by grace through faith.
They are saved by works. Christian people
can't just go through life saying, "I'm just
saved by grace. Praise the Lord, I don't have to
do anything." James said, "Faith without
works is dead". Dead faith won't save you! Our
spirits are saved by grace through faith. Complete, finished, once and for all, eternally
secure... *spiritually.* But you also have a soul,
and a body, and those are not saved in the same
manner.

9

2
WHAT IS RENEWING THE MIND?

And be not conformed to this world: but be ye transformed by the renewing of your mind, that ye may prove what is that good, and acceptable, and perfect, will of God. (Romans 12:2)

Paul says, "Don't be conformed to this world". You can be saved, and still be conformed to the world. Many born again, tongue talking people still live, talk, walk, think, and act, just like the world. *And* they feel just like the world. They are no happier than the average alcoholic down in the tavern. In fact, the alcoholic might even be a little happier when he's drunk. They are Christians, but they are not enjoying Christianity. They are still conformed to the world.

Paul, in writing the book of Romans, wasn't writing to sinners. He was writing to the church at Rome. They were born again, Spirit filled believers. Men and women who were operating in the gifts of the Spirit. They knew Jesus as Lord, and Savior, baptizer, and healer. Yet, he said, "Don't be conformed to the world".

If you are still depressed, you are conformed to the world. If you still feel bad, you are conformed to the world. If you're uptight, you are conformed to the world. If you're afraid, you're conformed to the world. If you can't look at people eye to eye, and talk to them, and love them, and share with them openly; you are conformed to the world. If you are still involved with masturbation, fornication, adultery, pornography, fantasies, etc.; you are conformed to the world. Paul said, *'Don't do that!'* Don't be conformed to the world, and he goes on to tell you how.

But be ye transformed.

Transformed means 'metamorphosis'. The Greek word is, 'metamorpho'. It is a complete, and total change. It is ceasing to be one thing, and becoming another. A caterpillar goes through metamorphosis. He stops being a caterpillar, and becomes a butterfly. The change from a caterpillar to a butterfly is not just a little progression, it is a complete change. Metamorphosis doesn't mean just learning a little bit more.

Some people come to church because they want to learn a little bit. They want to add to what they have already. But they should come to church to change. They should become totally new people. Metamorphosis! Transformed!

How are you changed? How are you transformed? How can you become this totally new person? By the renewing of your mind. You are transformed by the *renewing of your mind.*

Remember, the mind is part of your soul. Your mind, or your soul, has to be transformed. It has to be renewed, it has to be changed.

You can enjoy salvation here on earth. You can enjoy being saved, *now*. You can receive the provision, and the blessings of God, right now. But, you have to renew your mind to be able to receive those blessings. He said, it's by the renewing of your mind. Look at the end of the verse. (Romans 12:2)

> That ye may prove what is that good, and acceptable, and perfect will of God.

The good, and acceptable, and perfect will of God. How can you do the perfect will of God? By renewing your mind, by changing your soul. Your soul must become totally different. John said, 'You will prosper, even as your soul prospers'. Paul said, 'You will do the will of God, even as your mind is renewed'. If you're not renewing your mind, then you are not doing the will of God in your life. You're not accomplishing what God has for you, because the only way you can do the will of God, is by renewing your mind. You have to work every day, every hour, to renew your mind. You have to be in a constant process of changing your way of thinking, to be able to do the will of God.

Paul shows us in that verse that renewing the mind is a progressive change.

That ye may prove what is that good,
and acceptable, and perfect will of God.

Some of you have renewed parts of your mind,
and you're doing the *good* will of God. You're
not really enjoying all of it, but you are doing a
part of it. It's *good* that you're saved. It's *good*
that you're filled with the Holy Ghost. It's *good*
that you speak with new tongues. It's *good*
that you are doing the things you are. But, he
said, if you keep on growing in the renewing of
your mind, you can do the *acceptable* will of
God. You can enter farther into the blessings,
farther into the prosperity, farther into the
benefits of Christianity. And if you continue to
renew your mind, you will get to the place
where you will do the *perfect* will of God. It's
good to be going to heaven, but I'd like to live
in heaven right now, on earth. I can enjoy the
fruits of heaven right now. Jesus said, 'That
will be done on earth as it is in heaven'. You
can have heaven here on earth. But you have
to renew your mind to have that. You have to
progress in the things of God to have that.

Look at James 1:21.

Wherefore lay apart all filthiness and
superfluity of naughtiness, and receive
with meekness the engrafted word,
which is able to save your souls.

He didn't say, your soul is saved by making
Jesus your Lord. He said, you have to receive
with meekness the 'engrafted word'. And he

said that to Christians. He said, 'Receive with meekness the engrafted word, which is able to save your souls'. This is written to people that are already born again. The Amplified Bible says,

> So get rid of all uncleaness and the rampant outgrowth of wickedness and any humble, gentle, modest spirit receive and welcome the word which emplanted and rooted in your hearts contains the power to save your souls.

Notice it says, the Word contains the power. But it won't work unless you renew your mind. The Word contains the power, but the power is not released unless you use your will, and renew your mind to make it work. If it just worked automatically, you could sit in church, go to sleep, and the Word would go into your head. You'd wake up with a whole new mind. But that doesn't work. You have to receive the Word, and then make it work by an act of your will. Change your thinking, renew your mind, and apply the Word of God in your life, and *then* the power will come to save your souls. Hebrews 10:38, 39 says,

> Now the just shall live by faith: but if any man draw back, my soul shall have no pleasure in him. But we are not of them who draw back unto perdition; but of them that believe to the saving of the soul.

You can draw back, and *give up* your salvation. He said, 'We're not a part of them who draw back into perdition, draw back into sin, draw back into negativity, draw back from the gift of salvation. We're of them who believe unto the saving of the soul'. That's an ongoing thing. That's a continual thing. Can you lose your salvation? No, you can't lose it, but you can draw back from it. You can leave it. You can reject it. Go to I Peter 1:9.

> Receiving the end of your faith, even the salvation of your souls.

The end of your faith, *is* the salvation of your soul. The beginning of your faith in Jesus, is when you were born again. "Whoever will call upon the name of the Lord shall be saved." But the end of your faith is the saving of your soul, the renewing of your mind. We need to go on from being born again to being transformed—metamorphosis—by renewing our mind. This is the saving of our soul—the end of our faith.

3
DO YOU NEED CHANGING?

Some time ago, the Lord gave me a very clear picture of what it means to renew your mind. Some friends of mine had a little baby boy. This little guy was so cute, and adorable, but every few minutes he had a situation that needed attention from Mom or Dad. He needed changing. *His diaper needed to be renewed.* Just think how it would be if Mom took a nice clean diaper, and put it over top of that old dirty diaper. She could sprinkle lots of powder around, and make it smell, and look real good, but of course you know, in just a few moments that cover up would be smelling. The problem is still there. Eventually the child would get a rash, or other problems.

This is what many Christians are doing in their minds. They're really not renewing, or changing their thoughts; they are trying to cover up, or hide the way they think, in hopes that it will some day go away. Of course it doesn't, so the result is, we have Christians being divorced, committing adultery, using drugs, committing crimes, being depressed, or even taking their own lives. The reason why is, those old thoughts were not dealt with. Eventually what is in their minds will come out. Proverbs 23:7 says,

> As a man thinketh in his heart, so is he.

Let's go back to our diaper illustration. What must be done first, is take off the dirty diaper, and clean up that little bottom. Once our little friend is clean and dry, we put on the clean diaper. So it is with renewing the mind. First we must realize we have some dirty thoughts, or thinking that is contrary to the Word of God. (This doesn't mean sexual thoughts only. It could be fear, doubt, worry, jealousy, etc.) Then we deal with those thoughts, not just cover them up. We confess whatever they are, according to I John 1:9,

> If we confess our sins, he is faithful and just to forgive us our sins, and to cleanse us from all unrighteousness.

Then we make the decision to change the way we think. We go to the Word, and find out how God wants us to think, and replace our old thinking with new thoughts from the Bible. Of course we know that our old habit will pop up again, or Satan will try to bring it back on us, but we resist it, and continue to think on our new thoughts. Philippians 4:8 tells us,

> Finally, brethren, whatsoever things are true, whatsoever things are honest, whatsoever things are just, whatsoever

things are pure, whatsoever things are lovely, whatsoever things are of good report; if there be any virtue, and if there be any praise, think on these things.

Fix your mind on these things ... It's just like our little boy. His diaper will be dirty again soon, and we must clean him up, and put another clean diaper on. It is an ongoing process. However, some day he will no longer need diapers. When we continue to renew our minds, eventually those thought patterns will be renewed, and not come back. We realize negative thinking, confess it, decide to change it, and replace it with God's thoughts. We'll never get to the place where we don't have to renew our minds anymore, because none of us will ever be perfect. Only God has perfect thinking. We will never be God, but we are to always seek to be as He is. Matthew 5:48 says,

Be ye, therefore, perfect, even as your Father, who is in heaven, is perfect.

If we ever get to the place where we stop changing the way we think, we will stagnate, and die. The Christian life is a constant process of growth. God is ever calling us to greater things. If we refuse the change, we stop walking with God, and dry up.

As we look in Church history, we see many great moves of God that stopped, and died after several years. The reason can be easily seen in the renewing of the mind. Those in the movement thought they had all God had to offer, and they did not continue to grow, and change. Soon they were out of the perfect will of God, because they had not been renewing their minds. The move of God in 1960, is not the same as in 1980. I know the cardinal doctrines of the Bible never change, but the way we minister those doctrines changes from generation to generation. Once we become set in our ways, and do not renew our minds, we stifle our own life.

It seems that those who are up in years have a harder time renewing their minds than young people. They feel they know some things, and it's time for everyone to listen to them. It's true that wisdom comes with years, but many elderly folks cut off their own success because they do not continue to grow, and change. In the church world, the business world, the entertainment world, etc., we see very clearly how important it is that we never stop changing, but continue to renew our minds.

The children of Israel give us a beautiful picture of how we must always be changing. Let's read Numbers 9:16-23.

> So it was always: the cloud covered it by day, and the appearance of fire by night. And when the cloud was taken up from the tabernacle, then after that the children of Israel journeyed; and in the place where the cloud abode, there the

19

children of Israel pitched their tents. At the commandment of the Lord the children of Israel journeyed, and at the commandment of the Lord they pitched; as long as the cloud abode upon the tabernacle they rested in their tents. And when the cloud tarried long upon the tabernacle many days, then the children of Israel kept the charge of the Lord, and journeyed not. And so it was, when the cloud was a few days upon the tabernacle, according to the commandment of the Lord they abode in their tents and according to the commandment of the Lord they journeyed. And so it was, when the cloud abode from evening unto the morning, and that the cloud was taken up in the morning, then they journeyed whether it was by day or by night that the cloud was taken up, they journeyed. Or whether it were two days, or a month, or a year, that the cloud tarried upon the tabernacle, remaining thereon, the children of Israel abode in their tents, and journeyed not; but when it was taken up, they journeyed. At the commandment of the Lord they rested in the tents, and at the commandment of the Lord they journeyed: they kept the charge of the Lord, at the commandment of the Lord by the hand of Moses.

Notice how over, and over the Lord emphasizes, "At the commandment of the Lord they abode, at the commandment of the Lord they abode, at the commandment of the Lord they journeyed". The people constantly had to be ready to go, or stay. They could never get settled in their ways, or comfortable where they were.

Just imagine what would have happened if one guy had said, "I've come far enough. I followed the Lord for twenty years, and this is where God wants me to stay." Within a matter of time, the cloud would move, and he would be left behind. All his friends and neighbors would have packed up, and moved on. His kids would be mad because their friends were gone, and his wife would be upset because her prayer group was gone. But he said, "We've come far enough. I've changed a lot, and I have the right to relax for awhile." Pretty soon the hot sun burns them, because the cloud of covering is gone, and the night freezes them because the pillar of fire is not there. Then the guy starts saying, "Lord, why did you let this happen? Why don't you answer my prayers?" You see folks, God is not the problem. God wanted him to be under the pillar of fire, or the cloud, and God wanted him to be with the rest of the nation. But because this guy wouldn't change, he wouldn't continue to go, and grow with God, he would not receive the life God had for Him.

We must continue to renew our minds, to continually change the way we think. We must continue to grow strong in the Word in order to live the kind of life God desires for us to have.

4
THE SOUL! WHAT IS IT?

The soul is your *mind,* your *will,* and your *emotions.* The soul realm is where Christians get into trouble. It is where your thinking, and reasoning takes place. What does the soul mean to you in your Christian life? The opening verse of the apostle John's letter contains some powerful insight into the successful Christian life, and the part that your soul plays in that success. III John 2 says,

> Beloved I wish above all things that thou mayest prosper and be in health, even as thy soul prospereth.

John was the oldest living apostle at the time this was written. He said, 'This is my number one prayer. I pray this above *everything else.'* Now it certainly wouldn't have a preeminent part in his prayer life, if it wasn't primary to the Christian life. He said, "I pray above all else, that you would prosper and live in health, even as your soul prospers."

The words 'even as', cause you to realize that the success in your life will be governed, or determined by your soul. The prosperity, the health, the abundance of your life, will be 'even as your soul prospers, and lives in abundance'. Even as your soul prospers, *or* doesn't prosper; your life *in general* will prosper, or not prosper.

The soul is something that has been very misunderstood. It is misunderstood because of a lack of knowledge, and because of wrong talking, and wrong teaching. It has been established that the initial work of salvation is a spiritual thing. Paul said, "If any man be in Christ he is a new creature." Is your body new? No! Is your head new? No! Your 'spirit' is new. He said, "Old things pass away, all things become new." Did that happen physically? No, it happened spiritually. Spiritually you became a new creature. Before you were born again, you were *dead* spiritually, but after you were born again, you became *alive* spiritually. *That* is the initial work of salvation. That is *spiritual salvation.* That is what you must do to have eternal life, and go to heaven. But *that's not all* that is included in salvation.

Salvation is an instantaneous thing, *and* it is also a *progressive* thing. You were 'spiritually' saved for all time the day you made Jesus the Lord of your life. You were spiritually recreated, you were spiritually placed into fellowship with God. You now have communion with the Holy Spirit, in your spirit. But...you were only born. You were a babe in Christ at that point. Remember I said that salvation is *progressive?* Well, the soul is the realm in which salvation progresses.

If you were born again, and were told that

you would spend eternity in heaven, but that was all being born again would do for you; then that means, although you were born again, you would continue to still be sick, still be miserable, still be depressed, still be fat, still be lazy, still mess up your family, still have no control over your body, still have no love flowing in your life. You can be born again, and *still be a mess*. But, salvation *does* progress in the soul realm.

I'm sure we've all heard someone say, or have said it ourselves, "We are believing for souls to be saved". That statement is wrong, and unbiblical. We can't believe for souls to be saved. A soul that is being saved, is one that is being changed, and renewed to the will of God progressively. If we were speaking Biblically correct, we would say, "We are believing for spirits to be saved." The soul does not change when we get born again. Our soul is still the same.

Many people think that the spirit, and the soul are the same thing, but let's take a look at what the Bible says about the spirit, and the soul. I Thessalonians 5:23 says,

> And the very God of peace sanctify you wholly; and I pray God your whole spirit and soul and body be preserved blameless unto the coming of our Lord Jesus Christ.

See, it says the *whole* man: spirit, and soul,

and body. Notice the word *wholly*. It's not 'holy'. It's *wholly,* meaning 'every part', 'completely', 'all of you'. And Paul finished the verse by telling us every part, the WHOLE of our lives that must be sanctified.

You need to be sanctified spiritually; that takes place when you are born again. You need to be sanctified soulishly (mind, emotions, and will); that takes place when you work on yourself *throughout* your Christian existence. And you need to be sanctified physically. Spirit, soul, and body.

The spirit, and soul are not the same. If the spirit, and the soul were the same, he would have said, 'I pray that your spirit, and your body be preserved'. But he didn't. He distinguished between the two. The spirit, and the soul are two different things.

Hebrews 4:12 says,

> For the word of God is quick, and powerful, and sharper than any twoedged sword, piercing even to the dividing asunder of soul and spirit.

The Word of God divides the soul, and the spirit. If they can be divided, they cannot be the same, and the Word of God *will* divide them. But notice this also, the soul and the spirit function so closely together, that the Word is the only thing that can differentiate between the two.

Let's take a look at the characteristics of the

soul. The soul contains our personality, and we all have different personalities. That's a soul-ish difference. The soul contains the element of sense. Our senses operate in our soul. Our senses feed information to our soul, and our soul then makes decisions according to our senses. Our soul contains our emotions. Emotions are what we usually call feelings, and they change according to what is going on around us. Our soul relates to the elements, and rudiments of the world. It's contact is the natural realm. Our will is also contained in our soul. Our will, is our power to make decisions. Our power to change. Those characteristics all make up the soul. They are all a part of the soul realm.

Paul said that you need to be sanctified soul-ishly. That's something you have to work on continuously, because your mind, your emotions, your will, your senses, your personality, your desires *do not* instantly change. For example, if you smoked cigarettes before you were saved, most likely you will keep on smoking cigarettes after you are saved. Your spirit has been recreated and is new, but you still have the same desires. Your soul is still the same. The soul has desires that don't change instantly. They must be changed, and worked on progressively.

The soul contacts two realms. In Genesis 2, the Bible said that God breathed into man the breath of life. He breathed into that body, which He molded, the breath of life. Then it said, 'man became a living soul'. The soul was that natural life which took place when the spirit, and the flesh came together. So now the soul has become the intermediary, or the mediator between the body, and the spirit. Or you could say between the spirit world, and the flesh world. In other words, your spirit receives things from God; your body receives input from the world, and the soul stands in between them. The soul is the go between.

Now the soul can respond, and react to either one. The soul can follow the body; like when a person is fat. The body never wants to get up, and exercise, and keep itself strong, and healthy, because the body is always bent on destruction. The flesh wants to destroy itself because there is sin in the body. The body wants to be lazy, and fat. The soul can obey the body when it wants to lay down, and take a nap in the middle of the day, but at the same time, the spirit is saying, "No! I'm not going to submit to that. I have work to do. I have things to do. I want to pray. I want to get this job done. I want to study the Word." So the soul could say, "That's right spirit, I'll agree with you. Body, you be quiet, and get to work." But you see, that's your choice, and it all takes place in the soul realm.

Each one of you makes your decisions, makes your choices, establishes your whole life from your soul. That's why John said, 'You will prosper and live in health, even as your soul prospers'. If your soul is making the wrong choices, and deciding on the wrong things, and following the flesh, you are not going to prosper. You are going to get out of shape spiritually, mentally, and physically. But if the soul chooses to follow the spirit, chooses to obey the Word, chooses to believe that which is right, and chooses to obey the truth; then you will prosper, and live in health. It's all based on your soul.

Everything that comes from the natural man, comes into the soul. Everything that comes from the spirit man, comes into the soul. The Spirit of God will speak to the human spirit, and it will come to your soul. You then either accept it, or reject it. The world will speak to your body, and it will come to your soul. You then either accept it, or reject it.

The world will talk to your body sometimes, and it might say, "You're sick. You have the flu." Your soul receives that information, and it relays the message. It says, "Your body says it's sick. There is pain in here, and you need to go get some medicine." Now, your soul can respond to that message, *or* it can listen to your spirit which says, "No! Your body is not sick. By His stripes you were healed. The Spirit of God dwells in this body, and the Bible says, the Holy Spirit that raised Jesus from the dead makes this mortal body alive. Soul, don't accept that message from your body, send back this message. 'Body, you're well in the name of Jesus'." Now *you* have the choice.

Some people walk into the church saying, "Oh, I feel so bad. I'm so low." You understand,

and can see clearly that their soul is receiving messages from their bodies, and it is believing every word their body says. Then there are other folks who come in saying, "Hallelujah, how are you doing brother? Glory to God." Now you understand, and can see clearly that his soul is receiving messages from the spirit man, and it's believing everything the spirit says. You can accept, or you can reject every message that comes to your soul from either the body, or from the spirit.

You need to be aware, and understand something. If your soul is messed up, every time the spirit gives you a message, you will mess it up before you can put it to use. For example, theoretically, if I teach you what I do to be happy, you should be able to go, and do the same thing, and be happy. God's no respector of person's. That means, if it will work for me, it will work for you. But, I can tell you something that I do that enables me to walk in peace, and joy, and be victorious, and successful, in every area of life, but it may not work for you. Because, by the time it gets into your body, and your body feeds it from the ear into the soul, and your soul works on it a little while, you twist it all up. You turn it all around, get it all confused, and then you don't receive what I put out. You receive some garbled message that won't do you any good, or you just won't use it.

The Holy Ghost has awakened many of you in the morning at a certain time, and said, "Get up, and start praying." That thought hit your head, and went straight to your soul.

Then your soul started to work. "Well now, don't get in too big a hurry. You wouldn't want to jump out of bed and throw your back out. Just take it easy, and lie back for a few more minutes. Oh, doesn't this bed feel good? You're going to pray, don't worry, but just don't get too excited. Just another five minutes, and you'll still be able to pray." Pretty soon, "Well, you deserve another fifteen minutes." See, your soul is still working on you. You got the message from God twenty-five minutes ago, but you are in the process of scratching it completely out. "Well, you already wasted fifteen minutes, you may as well wait til you have barely enough time to get to work. Hit the 'snooze' again!" So finally the alarm goes off. You're racing through the house, with barely enough time to get dressed, get into the car, and get down the road. Then you wonder why, when you get to work, you make wrong decisions, and lose money. Or, you stick your hand in wrong places, and get cut, and hurt. The worst part of it all, is that you think, "Lord, why did *you* let this happen?" The Lord didn't let it happen. He was trying to get you up, and praying to take care of those things *before* they happened, but your soul rejected the voice of the spirit. In actuality, *you* caused those things to happen, not God. Your soul is messed up, and that's what's keeping you from receiving the blessings of Almighty God.

5
A PROSPEROUS SOUL
OR A POOR SOUL

I f you are not prospering, if you are not full of joy, and peace, and you are depressed; you need to wake up to the fact that your soul is in bad shape, and it is hurting you. Your spirit man is trying to grow. Your spirit man is trying to come out, and you are sitting there in your negative thinking, not wanting to change. *That* is keeping you from *your* prosperity, from *your* healing, and it's keeping you from *your* joy. If you are not prospering, you should know right away that your soul is not right. If you are sick, then your soul is sick. If you are sad, it's because your soul is sad. If you are having a problem in your life, the problem started in your soul, and is being manifested in other ways. The good news is that the soul can be renewed.

Your soul (your mind, emotions, and will) is the key to the success in your Christian life. If your soul is poor, your whole life will be poor. If your soul prospers, your whole life will prosper. You could say, if your mind, emotions, and will prosper, you will do the will of God. If they are poor, you will not do the will of God, as stated in Romans 12:2.

And be not conformed to this world: but be ye transformed by the renewing of your mind, that ye may prove what is that good, and acceptable, and perfect will of God.

Let's take a look at what constitutes a poor soul. Being poverty stricken in the soul realm is characterized by eight basic attitudes.

1) *Lack of knowledge of the Word of God.*
Hosea 4:6
My people are destroyed for lack of knowledge: because thou hast rejected knowledge, I will also reject thee, that thou shalt be no priest to me: seeing thou hast forgotten the law of thy God, I will also forget thy children.

2) *Being controlled by the desires of the flesh.* Such as money, food, sex, power, etc.
Romans 8:5,6
For they that are after the flesh do mind the things of the flesh; but they that are after the Spirit the things of the Spirit. For to be carnally minded is death; but to be spiritually minded is life and peace.

3) *Being weak, or indecisive, and choosing things contrary to the will of God.* Luke 10:42
But one thing is needful: and Mary hath chosen that good part, which shall not be taken away from her.

4) *Being undisciplined, and fantacizing on ungodly things.* II Corinthians 10:5
Casting down imaginations, and every high thing that exalteth itself against the knowl-

edge of God, and bringing into captivity every thought to the obedience of Christ.

5) *Refusing to change, and only seeking to prove yourself right, or defending yourself.* Romans 12:2

And be not conformed to this world; but be ye transformed by the renewing of your mind, that ye may prove what is that good, and acceptable, and perfect will of God.

6) *Being more concerned with things of this earth, than the things of heaven.* Colossians 3:2

Set your affection on things above, not on things on the earth.

7) *Allowing emotional feelings to decide how to act, instead of God's Word.* James 2:22

Seest thou how faith wrought with his works, and by works was faith made perfect?

8) *A mind that contains worry, fear, and negative thinking.* Philippians 4:8

Finally, brethren, whatsoever things are true, whatsoever things are honest, whatsoever things are just, whatsoever things are pure, whatsoever things are lovely, whatsoever things are of good report; if there be any virtue, and if there be any praise, think on these things.

With one, or more of these things going on inside you, you will be poor in the soul realm. According to III John 2, the prosperity of your life is based on the prosperity of your soul. If your soul is poor, it will affect every area of your life: marriage, business, faith, health, social life, etc.

Now on the other hand, there is the prosperous soul. The prosperous soul has seven basic characteristics.

1) *A mind that is ready to repent or change any thought at any time.* Romans 12:2
And be not conformed to this world, but be ye transformed by the renewing of your mind, that ye may prove what is that good, and acceptable, and perfect, will of God.

2) *A way of thinking that follows the Holy Spirit through the human spirit, not the flesh.* Romans 8:5,6
For they that are after the flesh do mind the things of the flesh; but they that are after the Spirit the things of the Spirit. For to be carnally minded is death; but to be spiritually minded is life and peace.

3) *A mind that meditates on God's Word regularly.* Psalms 1:2,3
But his delight is in the law of the Lord; and in his law doth he meditate day and night. And he shall be like a tree planted by the rivers of water, that bringeth forth his fruit in his season; his leaf also shall not wither; and whatsoever he doeth shall prosper.

4) *A mind that is disciplined to positive things with no fear, worry, or negativity.* Philippians 4:8
Finally, brethren, whatsoever things are true, whatsoever things are honest, whatsoever things are just, whatsoever things are pure, whatsoever things are lovely, whatsoever things are of good report; if there by any virtue, and if there be any

praise, think on these things.

5) *A will that is settled to do God's will, no matter what the cost.* Joshua 24:15

And if it seem evil unto you to serve the Lord, choose you this day whom ye will serve; whether the gods which your fathers served that were on the other side of the flood, or the gods of the Amorites, in whose land ye dwell: but as for me and my house, we will serve the Lord.

6) *A mind that is creative and sharp to follow the direction of the Holy Spirit.* Romans 8:14

For as many as are led by the Spirit of God, they are the sons of God.

7) *Emotions that are disciplined to the Word of God and do not control the way we live.* II Corinthians 5:7

For we walk by faith, not by sight.

As we train and discipline our mind, will, and emotions to the Word of God, prosperity will come. Not just money, but the kind of prosperity that counts with God. We will be men and women who raise up our children in the nurture, and admonition of the Lord. We will be leaders in our professions, and leading our peers to Jesus. We will have peace of mind, and strength in troubled times. We will succeed financially, so that we can give into the Kingdom of God. And, we will lead our communities, and nation to righteousness, and peace. These things will happen when our minds are disciplined, to God's way and God's Word.

Being a Christian is not all spiritual. As you've seen, you'll prosper even as your soul prospers. God gave you a mind to do many things on your own. The power of the soul is extraordinary, and few realize the great potential of it. Most of the Christian world has discounted the soul realm to be spiritual, but God never desired that. He said, "Be spiritual minded", and "Have a prosperous soul", but don't cut your head off. Use your mind for the glory of God. It's a part of God's tools for man's success. Often the world looks at Christians as a bunch of dumb dumbs. At times, we disregard all 'common sense', and pride ourselves on 'slip-shod' programs. I'm not saying we should seek to be intellectual wizards, but a prosperous soul is the basis for much of God's blessing. It will also go a long way to help us show the world we have something they need— the source of all prosperity—Jesus Christ.

6
WHAT IS A PROSPEROUS SOUL?

How does your soul prosper? What is the result of having a prosperous soul? What areas in your life will a prosperous soul affect? III John 2 tells us,

> Beloved, I wish above all things that thou mayest prosper and be in health, even as thy soul prospereth.

Once you find out how to have a prosperous soul, you will have opened the door to living in health, and financial prosperity.

John was writing this letter to a man by the name of Gaius. This man's soul was prospering, *and* he was living in health, *and* prospering financially. John goes on to tell us the reason why Gaius was prospering both in the soulish realm, and in the physical realm. Look at verses 3 and 4.

> For I rejoiced greatly, when the brethren came and testified of the truth that is in thee, even as thou walkest in the truth. I have no greater joy than to hear that my children walk in truth.

Gaius had a prosperous soul because the *truth* was in him; and he walked in the truth. Notice he didn't just say, the truth was in him. He went on to specifically point out the fact that he walked in the truth. The truth was in him, and he walked in the truth.

So many of you have the truth in you, but you don't walk in truth. You know the truth in your mind, but you don't live it. You hear it, but you don't do it. You've been taught the truth. For example, you have been taught how to pray in your understanding, and how to pray in the Spirit. You've been taught how to tithe, how to give, and you've been taught how to live ... but do you do it? Are you living it? James said, "He that heareth the Word, but doesn't do the Word, deceives himself."

What is deception? Very simply, deception is a lie. Your soul will prosper if you know the truth, and walk in it, but if you know the truth, and don't walk in it, you are deceived, or lying, according to James 1:23. The truth is not in you. You may know some things, but the truth really is not in you until you do it. When you know it, and do it, *then* the truth is in you. If the truth is not in you, you have lies in you, and you are deceived. Lies will keep your soul from prospering.

In order to walk in truth, we must first know what 'truth' is. Truth is the Greek word 'aletheia', and it literally means, 'unconcealed'. We could read that verse like this, "I have no greater joy than to hear that my children walk unconcealed." Truth also means, "the reality at the basis of appearance".

You can walk into church looking very holy, and spiritual but ... what is the reality at the basis of your appearance? Is the way you appear truth, or are you deceived? When the pastor stands up and says, "We're going to build a new church building", and out of your mouth comes, "Glory to God", what is the reality at the basis of your appearance? Do you give all that you can to fulfill that goal? Do you tithe regularly, *and* give over, and above your tithe to fulfill that goal, or do you give a little when you have an extra dollar or two, after you've done everything else you wanted to for yourself? Do you make sure that you got everything you wanted first, and go where you want to go, and do what you want to do first, and then maybe put a dollar, or two in the plate? You know, tip God. What is the reality at the basis of your appearance? Is the way you appear truth, or are you deceived? Are you a hypocrite?

You see, a hypocrite is not one who is in the world. A hypocrite is *not* one who says, "Well, I'm not going to go for that Christian stuff. I don't believe in God." That's not a hypocrite. That person is telling the truth. That's really where he is at. He doesn't want to have anything to do with it, and he lets you know about it. A hypocrite is a person who comes to church, nods his head at the Bible, but when he leaves the church, does not live the Bible. That person is a hypocrite.

The word 'hypocrite' came from the Greek

stage plays, where they would hold up different masks in the play to represent different characters. And that's what a lot of people do in church. They come into church smiling, and acting very holy. They lift up their hands a little bit, sing a couple choruses, but as soon as they get back into their cars, they put their church mask in the glove box, and pull out their worldly mask. They're back to their same old bad attitude, same old lousy way of thinking. They walk around all week with that mask on, and when they get back to church, they put it in the glove box, and pull out their church mask. *That* is a hypocrite. Jesus said, "Woe to you hypocrites!"

Truth means that you are unconcealed. The way you appear, is the way you really are. You should act in church, the same way you act at home. Or, you should act at home, the same way you act at church! If you don't want to do that, you shouldn't bother coming around the church. It is better to have five people who are committed to walk in the truth, than it is to have 5,000 who are hypocrites. That's why I want to put out the truth, and not some nice, cute things to pet people with. I want to get down to the truth, because it is the truth that enables your soul to prosper, and it's a prosperous soul that enables you to live a fruitful, free Christian life.

I realized a long time ago, that if you aren't going to go all the way with God's Word, then you might as well forget it. It is more miserable to be a lukewarm, hypocrite Christian, then to just go out in the world, and do your own thing. At least in the world you got a good feeling every once in awhile with drugs, or alcohol, or sex, or something. But when you know the truth, and you don't do it, you will be miserable all the time. God said, "I'd rather have you cold than lukewarm". Then He said, "Because you are lukewarm, I'm going to spew you out of my mouth."

Are you going to walk in the truth? Are you going to be unconcealed? Are you going to let the reality at the basis of your appearance, just come right out? If you will, that's when you will begin to prosper. That's when you begin to receive the prosperity that God has designed for your spirit, your soul, and your body. That's when you begin to walk in the abundant life that Jesus lived, and that Jesus gave to you.

Walking in the truth means, sometimes you have to uncover things you don't want to uncover. It means, sometimes you have to reveal some things you don't want to reveal. For example, some of you walk around, acting like such spiritual giants, and you don't want people to know that every time you open a magazine you go straight to the girly pictures. Now, you wouldn't go buy a pornographic magazine, but you can find enough naked girls in other magazines to take care of your little fantasy. But, you don't want to uncover that, you don't want to be real with that, because you've let everybody know how spiritual you are. You've let everyone think the Holy Ghost told you to do everything that you do. You don't want to uncover the real you. Until you can do that, you are not walking in truth. Until you deal with those things, until you can be real, and change those things, until you renew your mind so that you can walk in the truth, you will *never* be prosperous.

Depression is not truth. If you are depressed, you are walking in lies. If you walk around thinking about problems all the time, that's worry, and that's not truth. A lot of you have hostility within you. You are bitter, and mad, and upset with people. A lot of Christians are selfish, and only think about themselves. That's not truth! All these things are not truth, and you will never prosper with these things functioning in your life.

Satan is the master deceiver, and an area where he has so many Christians deceived, is in their "spiritual thinking". Actually, what it is, is a spiritual cop out. Rather than be responsible, and deal with the truth, it's easier to excuse their behavior.

In the world, if you have a behavioral problem, you explain it away as a disease. If it is a disease, you can't help it, and it's not your fault. For example, if you are an alcoholic, you have a disease. If you're a drug addict, you have a disease. If you are fat, you have a disease. You can't help it, you are sick. That's the way the world is, therefore, you are responsible for nothing.

Now in the church, you don't want to say you have a disease, because we will just lay hands on you, and get you healed. But you have another escape, you have a 'spirit'. "I don't know what it is Brother Treat. I think I have a glutton spirit. A glutton spirit keeps coming on me. I try to resist it, but it's too powerful for me." "Brother Treat, would you pray for me, and cast out the spirit of laziness in me?" As a Christian, you don't want to say you have a disease, you just say you have a spirit.

You need to realize that you have a soul, and *you* are responsible for what *you* do with that soul. You can know the truth, and walk in the truth, and be prosperous, *or* you can live a lie, and suffer under the depression, and the oppression of those lies. *You* are responsible. God gave *you* the choice. Look in Deuteronomy 30:19.

> I call heaven and earth to record this day against you, that I have set before you life and death, blessing and cursing: therefore choose life, that both thou and thy seed may live.

Notice that God said, it's all in front of you. Life and death, blessing and cursing, freedom and bondage, joy and depression, health and sickness. It's all in front of you. Everything either comes under the heading of life, or under the heading of death. There's only two choices; the kingdom of God, or the kingdom of the devil. Righteousness or sin. Health or sickness. Good or bad. And He said, "Therefore choose!"

What do you choose? Do you choose to be

righteous, or do you choose to be a sinner? Do you choose to think positive, or do you choose to think negative?

I realize that some of you have certain habits that you have been operating in for years, and years, and your minds have worked in certain ways for a long time, but you *can* change it. It might take some time. It might take you days, or weeks, or months, but you *can* change it, because God gave you a choice. That choice is your will power. That will is yours, and you can do with your will, *whatsoever* you desire. It's up to you. It's not a spirit, or a disease that makes us the way we are (although there are some this does apply to). It is the choices we make to walk in the truth, and have a prosperous soul that decide how our lives will be.

7
YOUR MIND
CONTROLS YOUR LIFE

Your mind is part of your soul. Let's take a look at Romans 8:5.

For they that are after the flesh, do mind the things of the flesh. (notice the word 'mind') They that are after the Spirit the things of the Spirit. For to be carnally minded is death; but to be spiritually minded is life and peace. Because the carnal mind is enmity against God: for it is not subject to the law of God, neither indeed can be. So then they that are in the flesh cannot please God.

You have flesh, and as long as you're in your body, you will have to deal with the flesh, or what is known as the 'sinful nature', the lower nature. Paul said it like this, 'I buffet my body daily to keep it under subjection'. He knew that his body would rise up, and cause even the great apostle Paul to go, and commit sin. But he said, 'I stay on top of my body. I make my body submit. I make my body obey, and I will not allow it to sin.'

You also have your spirit, which contains the

Holy Spirit. In between the flesh, and the spirit, you have your mind. Your mind can work both ways. Fleshly, and spiritually. Notice the Bible said, "They that are after the flesh do mind the things of the flesh. They that are after the Spirit, the things of the Spirit."

You have good things come into your mind, and you have bad things come into your mind. For example, you'll be sitting in the service, shouting 'Hallelujah', and the pastor will say, "We're going to take up an offering!" Out of your mind comes, 'Put in $100.00,' and you say, 'I rebuke you in the name of Jesus.' You have a choice. You can be carnally minded, or spiritually minded. The problem comes when you continually go back and forth.

So, what you do through study, discipline, confession, talking, tapes, books, the Bible, through every available method, is cause your thinking to be renewed. You no longer obey the dictates of the flesh, or the desires of the flesh, but instead stay over in the spirit man. That way you won't keep running back and forth.

It is amazing to me how quickly people can change from spiritual to carnal thinking. You can stand in church with your hands lifted up, praising God, and be shouting "Glory", and ten minutes later, walk right out the door, and come off with the worst attitude! You tell your spouse something that should never have come out of your mouth, and just be the ugliest thing in town! *Just that fast!* And it's all because of your mind. You choose the condition that your mind will be in.

Take a look at children. Children's minds change very quickly. Have you ever seen a little child just after they've learned to walk? They see something on the coffee table, and they head straight for it. You can just see them tearing that thing up. So you say, "No! Don't touch that." You pick them up, turn them around, and *immediately* they are going for something else. They are *just going,* because their minds are continually going.

Another thing children change very quickly, is their moods. Mood is another way of saying, their thinking. Children change their thinking, or their moods very quickly. They might come to you, and say, "Dad, will you take me down, and buy me a candy bar?" Their thinking is on candy. Now if you say, "You already ate three dozen cookies, you don't need any more candy", what happens? "I don't like you." Immediately, they are mad, and pouting, and depressed. They stomp around the house, kick the toy, don't want to do anything ... just plain MAD! Then you decide that even though they can't have any candy, you could take them to the park to play ... tears dry up, lip comes back in, smile comes back on their face, and "OH BOY!" Just that fast. They go from bad to good in a hurry. What happened? Their thinking changed. *That's all.*

There is no difference between children and adults, except that children are a little less trained, and intellectual. We as adults, act the same way. When something is going on we don't like, we think bad, or we act depressed, and we get down. When something is going on we really like, we act happy, and joyful, and fired up. It's all based on the way we think.

The spiritual mind, is the mind that is programmed, renewed, or set on the Word of God. How often does the Word change? Never. Jesus said, "Heaven and earth will pass away, but my Word will not". So the spiritual mind is controlled by the Word. If you are spiritually minded, you won't have any moods but good moods. You won't go up and down, because your mind is always on the Word, and the Word doesn't go up and down.

Today, you are more than a conqueror according to the Bible; just like you were yesterday in the Bible; just like you will be tomorrow in the Bible. It always calls us more than conquerors. You are victorious today, based on the Word of God; just like you were yesterday. Now you may say, "Yesterday I was down. Yesterday I was defeated." Yes, but the Word didn't say that, your unbelief said that. Your negative thinking said that. Your own ideas said that, based on the dictates of your flesh. The Bible, by the Spirit, said, 'You are victorious! You are an overcomer! You are a winner!'

The spiritual mind is programmed to the Word, and the Word *only*. Paul said, 'All the world can be going upside down, but we look not at the things which are seen. We look at the things that are unseen.' That's why a Christian can go through the middle of hell on earth with a smile. He's not affected by all those *things*, by all those worldly influences. He *doesn't care* about circumstances. He doesn't live according to circumstances. He is spiritually minded. He lives according to the Word, and to the Word only.

Any time you are depressed, any time you are full of fear, any time you worry, or 'think about something negative a lot'; that is your carnal mind. That is a mind that is submitted to the lower nature, to the things of the flesh. Remember your body, your flesh, your lower nature is controlling you right then. You are out of the spirit, and you cannot hear from the Holy Spirit in that condition.

You have to *make* yourself plug into the Word, plug into the Spirit. You have to get your mind programmed to the Spirit, to the Word, to the things of God, and get *off* of your problems. Get *off* of your misery. Get *off* of your depression. It's all based on what you set your mind on. Let's read that same verse, Romans 8:5, out of the Williams Translation.

> For people who live by the standards set by their lower nature, are usually thinking on the things suggested by that nature.

People say, "You can't be happy all the time." That's a low standard. "Well, not everybody can be well. Some people have to be sick. If people don't get sick, how are they going to die?" That's a low standard. People who live by the low standard, are usually thinking the things suggested by that nature. And, that's the sinful nature, the lower nature. But people who live by the standard set by the Spirit, the higher standard, are usually thinking the things suggested by the Spirit. It all comes back to their thinking. Paul said in Romans 8:6,

> To be thinking the things suggested by the lower nature means death.

Death comes in different degrees. You can be born again, and dying, in the sense that you are missing out on the abundant life. You're living in pain. You're living in poverty. You're fighting with your spouse. You have no joy. You have no love. You have no peace in your home. Those things are all a part of death. And that comes because you are thinking on the lower nature. Now, he says again,

> To be thinking the things suggested by the Spirit means life, and peace.

Did you know that you can be very religious, and follow the sinful nature? You can be very religious, quote scriptures, put on a holy act, and be in the sinful nature. Thinking on things of the flesh. Do you know how you can tell if you are in the sinful nature? When there is no peace around you. When there is no love flowing between you, and other people. Then, you are in the flesh. When there is no joy coming out of you, bubbling up out of you, you are in the flesh. That's the sinful nature.

The things of the Spirit, the spiritual mind, leads to life, and peace. You know you have a spiritual mind, when you know you are alive. Not just existing, but *full* of life, *full* of power, and *full* of peace. If you are without peace, your mind is messed up. The only time you lose your peace is when your thinking goes wrong. That's the only time you lose your peace. Any time you are worrying about the government, the stock market, the economy, the kids, the family, the school; that's when your thinking goes wrong. When your thinking is in line with the Spirit of God, and the Word of God, you have *peace every day.* You will have perfect peace all the time, and you will never lose it. Isaiah 26:3 says,

> Thou wilt keep him in perfect peace, whose mind is stayed on thee: because he trusteth in thee.

Notice it didn't say, whose mind comes on thee once in awhile. Most of us bump into God a couple times a week. Like when we come to church. We think about God a little bit, and sometimes we might accidently see a Bible, and it reminds us of the Lord, but we just sort of "bump" into Him. The Bible said, "He'll keep you in perfect peace, whose mind is stayed on thee." Not once in awhile ... *stayed* on thee.

How do you put your mind on God? I tried to put my mind on God one day. I tried to picture God. What does He look like? Then I remembered what John 1:1 says,

> In the beginning was the Word, and the Word was with God, and the Word was God.

What He looks like isn't important. When I keep my mind on His Word, I am keeping my mind on God. He'll keep me in perfect peace, as long as I keep my mind on His Word.

When situations rise up, and I look at a mountain of debt, or I look at a mountain of need; I keep my mind on the Word, *not* on the need. If someone comes along, and says to me, "Brother Treat, we are going to need $100,000 to put the roof on that building", I say, "Oh thank you Father, you supply all my needs according to your riches in glory, by Christ Jesus". If I start looking at the need, I'm going to lose my peace. I'm going to worry, and I'm going to figure out how I can sell you parking places, and rent you chairs, or something to get the money.

All that negative, panic thinking, and worry, comes from no peace! Keep your mind on the Word, and He will keep you in perfect peace. "All my needs are met according to His riches in glory, by Christ Jesus. I remember the Lord my God, not the problem. I remember the Lord my God, for it is He that giveth me the power to get wealth." (Deut. 8:18) Where your mind is, that's where your life is.

8
HOW TO GET YOUR MIND IN SHAPE

In the last few years, we have learned much about the function of our muscles. We know that if we don't exercise, our bodies will become weak, out of shape, and lazy. The heart also needs exercise. Thousands of people die from heart attacks every year because that muscle becomes weak from lack of exercise, and can no longer keep blood flowing.

Well, the mind is also a muscle. It must be exercised, and challenged, or it will become weak and lazy. The devil knows this, and in his attempts to kill, steal, and destroy, he has done all he can to stop people from thinking. Millions of people around the world today have no challenge, or spark in their lives. The greatest American past time, T.V. watching, is one example of a nonthinking society.

Most people don't have to think on their jobs, they just perform regular routines. If they go to church, they follow in the same rut everyone else has followed for years. T.V., movies, sports, and other things merely entertain, but never challenge. Although we still have great thinkers, entrepreneurs, creative people, and go-getters, as a whole, our minds are lazy.

Many of us have sat idly by while alcohol, drugs, divorce, abortion, pornography, and homosexuality have flooded our nation, and nearly destroyed our liberty. The apathetic attitude, or "lazy mind" syndrome, that Satan has spread through the land, has caused these things to come to pass. Thank God we are waking up, and change is beginning to take place.

As we look at three major past times in the U.S., we see they all steal creativity, and create a nonproductive, dull mentality: alcohol, drugs, and T.V. Of course there are good aspects of medical drugs, and T.V. information, but as a whole, they are not developing a nation of successful people. Our children are spending much of their time seeing murder, fights, sexual affairs, or car chases. When they don't like the programming, they can shoot at space ships, or chase demons on the video game. All of these things bring an apathetic attitude, and character that is less than Godly. Even in our public schools secular humanist teachers use a style of teaching that stops children from developing their minds and causes them to be lulled into humanist philosophies.

As Christians, we need to exercise our minds, stir ourselves up, and be sharp to labor with our Lord. Proverbs 10:15 teaches that a lazy mind leads to poverty, and destruction. God is looking for sharp, clear thinking, creative people He can lead to victory on this earth. There are millions of inventions still to be developed, hundreds of business opportunities still to be had, and thousands of ministry possibilities that God is waiting to share with us. The lazy mind will never see, or receive the blessing of it. Only the clear, disciplined, active mind will handle it.

In the early part of the 1900's, a man in the U.S. government tried to close the patent office, because he believed there would be no more inventions. He saw no reason to spend federal money to keep that office open when everything had already been invented that would ever be in the world. Since then, the knowledge, and inventions of the world have doubled many, many times. His lazy mind could see no more, but thank God others did, and we have the benefits today.

As Christians, we should be meditating, asking, seeking, and knocking for ways to lead our families, build our churches, and influence our world. Whatever our sphere of influence, there is more we can do, if we will use the tools God has given us.

Satan is no dummy. He has developed strongholds that blind our minds, and stop us from proving the perfect will of God. II Corinthians 10:4,5 says,

> For the weapons of our warfare are not carnal, but mighty through God to the pulling down of strongholds; casting down imaginations, and every high thing that exalteth itself against the knowledge of God, and bringing into captivity every thought to the obedience of Christ.

In the work of the ministry, I've found the greatest stronghold in people's minds to be, mental laziness. I don't mean going to work, mowing the grass, or helping out at church (although there is an abundance of laziness in these areas too). I'm speaking of *mental laziness*.

The average American person has so much outside stimulation that his mind has become lazy, and inefficient. In days gone by, men and women occupied their time with work, fellowship, teaching, training, and other aspects of life. Today we allow someone else to fill our time. Several hours a day are often filled with television programming. This creates mental stagnation. Our minds do not have to work. We just sit there like zombies, and allow the world to pass before us.

Young people are a good example of the effects of mental laziness. Many grow up with T.V. as a mother, father, and babysitter. When it comes time for school, their minds are uncoordinated, and simple learning becomes difficult. Studies show that many high school graduates do not have the basic skills of reading, writing, and mathematics.

Another sign of mental laziness is drug, and alcohol abuse. Rather than use their minds to solve problems, get answers, or enjoy living, people just check out. They pour some form of poison in their system to pacify, and entertain them rather than dealing with reality. After years of this, the mind is totally incapacitated.

Rather than seeking for a way to learn more skills, or improve their life, people, in general, are lazy. A T.V. program, a movie, or a "joint" is more interesting than renewing the mind. In our country today, there is a great need for creative people. People with fresh minds, vivid imaginations, creative abilities. These are the kinds of people who started the United States of America, and made it the great country it is today. The conveniences of electricity, automobiles, computers, and T.V. did not come through lazy, stagnant minds.

All of this mental laziness hurts the spiritual life. Most Christians do not take the time to dig into the Word of God, find answers to problems, and grow in the knowledge of the truth. They just go to church, sit in a pew, and accept anything the preacher says. It doesn't matter that he is just saying what he heard in some seminary, or read from a book. It doesn't matter that there is no anointing of the Holy Spirit, and no signs, or wonders. They just sit there, half asleep, and half confused. This is true all over our world today. I know there are some who are motivated, seeking, and hungry for truth, but the vast majority are mentally lazy. When you ask the average Christian how they study the Bible, they usually get up tight, grin, and give you some feeble excuse. The truth is, their minds are lazy, and they don't do anything. If you don't study for them, and spoon feed them, they'll get nothing.

Mental stagnation hurts our prayer lives, also. Have you ever sat down to pray, and after five minutes your mind had wandered in ten different directions, and you forgot what you needed to pray about? This is why many Christians don't pray more than five minutes. Their minds are so undisciplined, and out of control, that they *can't* pray for a prolonged period of time.

We must attack mental laziness, and drive it out of our lives. The only way to do this, is by renewing the mind. Instead of letting the T.V., a movie, or a book do all our thinking for us, we must begin to use our minds to seek out truth, and grow. Discipline is the name of the game. Instead of reading a chapter of the Bible, and forgetting what we read before we get to work, we need to do some meditating on what we read.

Take time to think about it. Ask yourself questions about it. Imagine the setting of the story, or the meaning of the message. You may only read one verse, but spend twenty minutes thinking on it, and you'll get more out of it than if you read a whole chapter. At first it will seem very difficult, and your mind will seem uncontrollable, but through consistent effort, your mind will be renewed, and you will drive out mental laziness. With the help of the Holy Spirit, and the power of God's Word, it is possible for every person to be sharp, creative, and mentally alive. With a renewed mind, you will enjoy all that God has to offer.

9
CONTROLLING YOUR THOUGHTS

Many people have no idea what goes thru their minds minute by minute. Doctors say we have over 10,000 thoughts a day, and yet to tell someone what we've been thinking would be very difficult.

Satan is aware that our mind is the arena of success. This is where the battle is fought. He has been working overtime to fill our minds with negativity, and will bring some of the most outlandish thoughts that could be imagined. Sometimes we may wonder where the thoughts came from. It is our enemy bringing negative thoughts to keep us from being the best.

Your eyes see negative advertisements, negative programs, alcohol, cigarettes, etc. Your ears hear negative words, music about defeat, misery, sickness, sex, etc. You are constantly receiving input to your mind. Now if you accept those thoughts, and begin to meditate on them, they will become a part of your *own* thinking, and eventually bring destruction on you. Proverbs 23:7 says,

For as he thinketh in his heart, so is he.

If you only go to church once a week, and hear the Word for 20 to 60 minutes, the negative input you receive is much greater than the positive. Out of 168 hours in a week, you may sleep 49 hours, so that leaves 119 hours to have thoughts going through your mind. If the only Word you receive is one church service (as is the case for most Christians), then you have 118 hours of carnal thinking to one hour of Word input. Even if you take off two hours a day for praying, or reading the Word, and thinking on positive things, you still have 104 hours of negative against 15 hours of positive. That's why God told Joshua to meditate the Word day and night. He had to override the input of Satan with the input of the Word of God. You will have to limit what comes into your senses, to get your mind under control, and be spiritually minded. A mind that is full of news, T.V., movies, rock and roll, worry, and other worldly input will never please God, or receive His blessings.

You need to realize, what you set your mind on will come to pass in your life. Look at Mark 7:20-23.

> That which cometh out of the man, that defileth the man. For from within, out of the heart of men, proceed evil thoughts.

Notice the first thing that comes out is *thoughts*. The first thing that defileth a man is *thoughts*.

Adulteries, fornications, murders, thefts, covetousness, wickedness, deceit, lasciviousness, an evil eye, blasphemy, pride, foolishness: All these evil things come from within, and defile the man.

We have been blaming the "evil spirit" which has come upon us for the way we think, and act, but it's not the spirit coming on us, it's what's coming from *within* us. That's what defileth the man. What's in your head? That's what's defiling you. That's what's messing up your life. If you would keep your mind on the Word, you wouldn't have trouble. There is no evil spirit on you. The trouble comes from *within* you. The Paraphrased Version puts it like this:

It is the thought life that pollutes. For from within out of man's heart comes evil thoughts of lust, theft, murder, adultery, wanting what belongs to others, wickedness, deceit, ludeness, envy, slander, pride, and all other folly.

All these vile thoughts come from within. They are what pollute you, and make you unfit for God. It's not the 'spirits' out there in the world that are messing you up. It's not the diseases in the world that are messing you up. *It's the thought life that pollutes.*

As the pastor of a large church, I've seen

many situations where a man or woman thought everything was going fine in their relationship with their spouse, and then one day the spouse disappears. They say, "But Pastor Treat, everything was so good. I know he/she loved me!" But the fact remains, they had been allowing Satan's attack to enter their mind, and eventually they did what they had been thinking about. Take heed, *if you think about something long enough, you will do it.* As a man thinketh in his heart, so is he.

It's the thought life that keeps us unfit for God. It's the thought life that allows all folly to come on us. Any foolishness, any sin that comes into our lives, is because of our own thoughts. "But Brother Treat, I was tempted, and I couldn't resist." The Bible says, God will not allow you to be tempted beyond what you are able to handle. If you are doing the things you were tempted with, it's because you have allowed those temptations to become a part of your thinking. The temptation is not the problem. You have the ability to overcome it. It's the way you think that has to change. The New International Version says,

> What you set your mind on is what you live.

If you set your mind on the flesh, you will live according to the flesh. If you set your mind on the Spirit, you will live according to the Spirit.

That's why the Father told Joshua, in Joshua 1:8,

> This book of the law shall not depart out
> of thy mouth; but thou shalt meditate
> therein day and night, that thou mayest
> observe to do according to all that is
> written therein: for then thou shalt
> make thy way prosperous, and then
> thou shalt have good success.

He wanted his mind to be on the Word day and night.

To meditate means, 'to ponder, imagine, think, mutter, or talk to oneself'. You see, as long as Joshua kept his mind on God's Word, he could do what God wanted him to do. He would prosper, and have good success. You cannot prosper, and succeed (or as the Hebrew says, 'deal wisely with the affairs of life') unless you keep your mind on the things of God. If you have a "loose wig", or a "scatter brain", forget it. You'll always be in and out of circumstances that you do not desire. Your thoughts must be disciplined to the Word of God for success, and prosperity to be yours. Psalms 1:1-3 says,

> Blessed is the man that walketh not in
> the counsel of the ungodly, nor standeth
> in the way of sinners, nor sitteth in the
> seat of the scornful. But his delight is in
> the law of the Lord; and in his law doth
> he meditate day and night. And he shall
> be like a tree planted by the rivers of
> water, that bringeth forth his fruit in
> his season; his leaf also shall not

64

wither; and whatsoever he doeth shall
prosper.

Here again, the Father is instructing you to
keep your mind on His Word. It is to be day and
night. That means all the time, for if it's not
day, it's night, and your mind should be on the
Word at both times. Now I understand you
have to think about your job, or family at different times, but the regular thoughts of your
mind must be on the Word. If you'll keep your
mind on His Word, you'll be like a strong tree.
Satan won't be able to blow you down. You'll
bring much good fruit for the kingdom. You'll
not wither or fail, and whatever you do will
prosper. That's good news. Isaiah 26:3 says,

> Thou wilt keep him in perfect peace,
> whose mind is stayed on thee: because
> he trusteth in thee.

When you become spiritually minded, success
is yours.

You need to begin to rise up in your mind.
Get your mind working in a positive way, then
the rest of your life will follow along. Think of
yourself as the *best*. Don't condemn yourself.

So often when you've heard good teaching,
instead of saying, "Glory to God, I'm glad I
learned that today", you say, "I knew I was no
good. I knew my head was messed up. I'm so
stupid. Why didn't I know that before?" Stop
beating yourself. Instead say, "Thank God I
got a hold of it now. I'm glad I learned about my

thinking. Maybe I *had* 'stinkin thinkin', but that's the end of it for me. Maybe I used to have 'hardening of the attitudes', but I'm going to get them changed." Don't condemn yourself, because as you think, so are you. Look at Colossians 3:1.

If ye then be risen with Christ, seek ...

If you are a Christian, if you are born again, if you are risen with Christ, if you call yourself a child of God, then you have to do this: *SEEK*. What does seek mean? Seek means, you search for it, you look for it, you go for it, you look *diligently* for it.

> Seek those things which are above, where Christ sitteth on the right hand of God. Set your affections (mind, thinking) on things above, not on things on the earth. (Colossians 3:1,2)

Do you set your mind on things above? Do you wake up in the morning thinking about the fact that God has redeemed you from destruction? Do you set your mind on the fact that Jesus is living in you right now? Do you set your mind on the fact that greater is He that is in you than he that is in the world? Do you set your mind on the fact that those who are sons of God, are led by the Spirit of God? You have to say, "Mind, this is what you are going to think on right now. You're going to think on this part of the Bible."

You have to make your mind think what you want it to think. You have to capture your thoughts, because your mind will think on whatever you let it think on. If you let your mind think on the newspaper, or magazines, if you listen to the news report on the radio, and watch a couple of hours of T.V. every day, you've spent two or three hours pumping negative, worldly things into your head. Colossians 3:1-2 in the Paraphrased says,

> Since you became alive again, when Christ arose from the dead, now set your sights on the rich treasures and joys of heaven where he sits beside God in the place of honor and glory. Let heaven fill your thoughts. Don't spend your time worrying about things down here.

I know the Bible is true. I know the Word of God is true. I let that fill my thoughts. Think on things above, not on things on the earth. That's how I get peace, peace, wonderful peace, coming down from the Father above.

To help us in our spiritual thinking, the Lord told us exactly what to think on. Look at Philippians 4:8. Paul was teaching some powerful truth in this verse.

> Finally brethren, whatsoever things are honest, whatsoever things are just, whatsoever things are pure, what-

soever things are lovely, whatsoever things are of good report; if there be any virtue, if there by any praise, think on these things.

Think on these things. That's *all* you should be thinking about. That means you can't worry about your kids. That means you can't worry about your money. That means you can't think about yourself. "I'm so no good. I'm so fat. I can't do anything right." You can't think about that anymore. That is not a good report, and that is not lovely thinking. You must only think on those things which line up with this verse. He said, "Think on these things". If it's not true, honest, just, pure, lovely, of good report, virtuous, and worthy of praise, don't think about it. One translation says, "Carefully consider *only* these things."

Do you know why the devil comes to us with all kinds of information, feeding us with things we can fix our minds on? He knows if he can keep our minds fixed on negativity, on evil, on bad reports, that we will live that way, and we'll be ineffective for God. That's why Satan has reports several times a day, telling us all the bad news, so he can keep our minds fixed on evil.

But God makes things so simple. He gave a complete list of what to think on, nothing more, and nothing less. All you have to do is set your mind on these things. Let's read that verse again from the Amplified Bible.

For the rest, brethren, whatever is true, whatever is worthy of reverence and is honorable, and seemly, whatever is just, whatever is pure, whatever is lovely and lovable, whatever is kind and winsome and gracious, if there is any virtue and excellence, if there is anything worthy of praise, think on and weigh and take account of these things—fix your minds on them.

Notice it said, *"Fix your mind on them".* This is an eternal process we have to be involved with. A process of renewing our minds. Thinking on those things which God directs us to think on. Think on nothing else. Not our worries, not our cares, not our fears, not our problems, but think on *these* things.

Think about the answers, and the problems will be left behind. If you think about the problems, they'll only get bigger. Sometimes when you pray, all you think about is your problem. You should be asking God, and believing for answers, and all you're meditating on are the problems, and confessing them out of your mouth. You need to renew your mind, and think on those things which are true, and pure, and lovely, etc.

Look over into II Corinthians 10:4.

For the weapons of our warfare are not carnal, but mighty through God to the pulling down of strongholds. Casting down imaginations, and every high thing that exalteth itself against the knowledge of God, and bringing into captivity every thought to the obedience of Christ.

You are in a war, and you have weapons to fight the battle with. But it's not a physical war. It's not a fleshly war. You fight your warfare in the spiritual realm. The way you do that, is by casting down imaginations. What is an imagination? What do you do when you imagine? You *think!* So he says, cast down thoughts, or thinking. Any time you have a thought that exalts itself against the knowledge of God, you have to cast it down. What does that mean? Every time a thought comes into your head, that is contrary to the knowledge of God, the Bible, you have to cast it down.

When the thought comes to your head, "Oh, you're sick, you'd better go lie down", the Bible says, "With His stripes you were healed", so cast that thought down. "I'm not sick, I'm well in Jesus' name." The thought comes to you, "You're going to lose your job, and you're not going to be able to pay your mortgage. Your house is going to be repossessed, and you're not going to be able to provide for your family." Cast that thought down. The Bible said, "My God shall supply all your need according to His riches in glory." Cast that worry down, because God will take care of your needs. Casting down imaginations, and *every,* not just some, but *every thing* that exalts itself against

70

the knowledge of God, and bringing into captivity every thought.

Do you know that you can control every thought? I didn't believe that for a long time. I thought it would be impossible to control my head. But I kept on thinking on things that are pure, and lovely, and just, and good, and honest, and of good report.

You too can control every thought, or the Lord wouldn't have told you to do it. You can capture every thought, or Jesus would not have put it in the Bible. The fact that He told you to do it, let's you *know* that you can. God is just, and He never tells you to do anything you cannot do. It will take some work. It will take some time. It will take some effort, but you *can* capture every thought, and make it obedient to Christ.

Who is Christ? Christ Jesus is the Word.

> In the beginning was the Word. The Word was with God, and the Word was God. (John 1:1)

Jesus is the Word of God. When your thoughts are submitted to the Bible, they are submitted to Jesus Christ. When you think only on those things which are in line with the scripture, then you are submitted to Christ. Remember Jesus said, "I have come that you may have life, and that you may have it more abundantly." Abundantly is superior in quality, and super abundant in quantity. That's what you will have when you get every thought under subjection; captured for the Lord Jesus Christ.

10
CHANGE BRINGS SUCCESS AND PROSPERITY

One thing that stops all growth in the spirit, and soul realm, is a defensive, "don't want to change" attitude. An attitude is simply a way of thinking, and very few Christians have an attitude of growth and change. It takes change to grow, and it takes growth to walk with God. Most of us are busy defending what we are doing now, rather than looking to change for tomorrow. We say we want to learn, but learning is not changing.

Learning is like the heathen man who heard about Jesus, and so accepted Him; adding Jesus to all his other gods. Changing is giving up what we now have, and gaining something new. There are situations where learning is necessary, but there are also times when change is necessary. History points out that God usually uses a whole new people to start His next move because the old movement refuses to change. Proverbs 9:7-9 says,

> He that reproveth a scorner getteth to himself shame: and he that rebuketh a wicked man getteth himself a blot.

Reprove not a scorner, lest he hate thee: rebuke a wise man, and he will love thee. Give instruction to a wise man, and he will be yet wiser: teach a just man, and he will increase in learning.

Notice the scorner, or wicked man does not want to be instructed, corrected, or reproved. He thinks he's right, and defends his position. He goes so far as to make those who try to correct him look bad. When you confront this type of person, you end up bringing problems on yourself. The wicked man hates people who try to instruct him. He feels they are against him, and hardens his heart. Proverbs 12:15

The way of a fool is right in his own eyes: but he that hearkeneth unto counsel is wise.

A wise man welcomes correction, and instruction. He wants to learn, and change, and loves those who help him. Wise men get wiser through challenge, and confrontation. Proverbs 10:8 says,

The wise in heart will receive commandments: but a prating fool shall fall.

Again we see wise men accepting confrontation, but fools wanting to be right, and going their own way. Proverbs 11:14 tells us,

> Where no counsel is, the people fall: but
> in the multitude of counsellors there is
> safety.

We all need to have a multitude of counsellors around us. A one man show, or person who cannot be confronted will always fall. It may take awhile, but they will fall. Often we Christians try to hide behind spirituality to avoid the counsel of others. We'll say, "The Lord told me..." or, "I feel led...", hoping that everyone will just agree, and things will work out the way we want them. I'm amazed at how many things the Lord supposedly told people to do that have failed miserably. It's obvious there would have been safety, had there been a number of counsellors.

Proverbs 12:1 is a strong word from the Lord.

> Whoso loveth instruction loveth knowledge: but he that hateth reproof is brutish.

Reproof means, 'rebuke, convict'. The person with this behavior is a brute. Loving instruction doesn't mean you just listen to a sermon once in awhile. It's easy to listen to a sermon, and then pass it off as irrelevant to you, or not applicable to your circumstance. You need to *love* direct, personal challenge, or confrontation on what you are doing. If it is not personal, and direct, it is not effective.

Many in the business world have found this truth, and we will find terms like "confrontive management", and others, being used. But in the Christian world, we have stayed away from these scriptural truths. Things that needed rebuking, or reproving, we've tried to pray away, or leave it up to the Lord. However, the Lord has left it up to us to help one another in a humble, and loving way, but also in a direct and honest way. Matthew 18:15-17 gives us New Testament reference for this.

> Moreover if thy brother shall trespass against thee, go and tell him his fault between thee and him alone: if he shall hear thee, thou hast gained thy brother. But if he will not hear thee, then take with thee one or two more, that in the mouth of two or three witnesses every word may be established. And if he shall neglect to hear them, tell it unto the church: but if he neglect to hear the church, let him be unto thee as an heathen man and a publican.

A willingness to change opens the door for people to bring counsel, and reproof that is a great blessing to every Christian. It is like sandpaper smoothing wood, and steel sharpening steel; the finish gets finer. Of course, the Lord is always convincing, and convicting by the Spirit, but He does much fine tuning through the body of Christ when we will let Him.

One thing we have to realize in this area, is that, reproof or confrontation does not feel good. The flesh reacts, our minds instantly begin to formulate defenses, and our emotions are hurt. Yet if we will open up, and learn to receive, the benefits are unlimited. It doesn't feel good, but it sure *is* good. Many times I've heard people say, "I don't have peace about what you said, so it can't be from the Lord". This sounds very spiritual, but it is totally unscriptural. Children don't feel peace in their heart about the rod, but God said use it to drive foolishness out. Likewise many followers of Jesus said, "This is a hard saying; who can hear it", and went back, no longer walking with Him. It didn't however, change Jesus' instruction to them. I'm quite sure the disciples didn't feel "peace" when Jesus told them, "The boy was not delivered because of your unbelief", but it was still the Word of the Lord. Truth is often a sharp, two-edged sword, but it always "makes us free".

The following scriptures are good examples of God's instruction, and His expectation of Christians in dealing with behavior that needs changing.
Proverbs 13:1

A wise son heareth his father's instruction: but a scorner heareth not rebuke.

Proverbs 13:18

Poverty and shame shall be to him that

refuseth instruction: but he that regardeth reproof shall be honoured.

Proverbs 15:10

Correction is grievous unto him that forsaketh the way: and he that hateth reproof shall die.

Proverbs 15:12

A scorner loveth not one that reproveth him: neither will he go unto the wise.

Proverbs 15:22

Without counsel purposes are disappointed: but in the multitude of counsellors they are established.

Proverbs 15:31-33

The ear that heareth the reproof of life abideth among the wise. He that refuseth instruction despiseth his own soul: but he that heareth reproof getteth understanding. The fear of the Lord is the instruction of wisdom; and before honour is humility.

Proverbs 6:23

For the commandment is a lamp; and the law is light; and reproofs of instruction are the way of life.

I don't think confrontation will ever "feel good", but if we will seek it, and receive it, our lives will be much richer. It is obvious God has made it a part of the Christian life, and we must not avoid it, but gain the benefits thereof.

11
HOW TO DO THE WILL OF GOD

For the born again, Spirit filled child of God, there is one major thing that hinders the fulfillment of the perfect will of God. *That is the mind.* The Word says,

> And be not conformed to this world: but be ye transformed by the renewing of your mind, that ye may prove what is that good, and acceptable, and perfect will of God. (Romans 12:2)

Many, many Christians are still conformed to the world. Conformed means 'molded'. Therefore, they cannot "prove" the will of God. A Christian who is conformed to the world, is one who still "thinks" like an unborn again person. His life is based on his feelings, his experience, the economy, the government, his job, or some other natural element.

A Christian who has been "transformed by the renewing of his mind" bases his life on the Word of God. His feelings, experience, or any other circumstance does not change what he believes, or how he acts. The Word is his foundation, and guide.

This is a very hard thing for most people to

grasp. We have been trained for so long to base our lives on how we feel, or on experiences. But this is very dangerous. All Satan has to do is serve us a few negative experiences, or defeats, and we are finished for the rest of our days. We base our whole lives on a negative circumstance, and so everything we do is bound for failure.

Preachers are a good example of this. I've heard many talk of all the people they've prayed for who have not been healed, or have died. So now they "know", and "believe" that healing is not for everyone. Their faith is based on their experience, *not on the Word.* This is wrong. It wouldn't matter if there had been no one healed by the power of God since 100 AD, the Word is still the same. "By His stripes ye were healed". (I Peter 2:24)

We are not here to preach, and believe our experiences, or testimonies, but rather the Word of God. If my circumstances become my foundation, I no longer need a Bible. This is what has happened to many Christians. They don't believe in tongues, healing, etc., or they believe these things are not for all, because of experiences. The renewed mind stays with the Word, no matter what the circumstances. Someone wisely said, *"I'm not moved by what I feel, or see. I'm moved by what I believe. And I believe the Bible."*

The word renew, in the Greek, is "Anakainoo". It means, 'to make new', or 'to change your thinking to God's thinking'. Isaiah 55:8,9 says,

For my thoughts are not your thoughts, neither are your ways my ways, saith the Lord. For as the heavens are higher than the earth, so are my ways higher than your ways, and my thoughts than your thoughts.

We must renew our thoughts for God's thoughts. His are higher, and better. I like to look at this like an exchange. I'm exchanging my way of thinking for God's way. I take back the old, and receive the new.

It's like when I purchase a piece of clothing, such as a tie. If it has a flaw in it, I want to exchange it. The first thing I must do, is realize I have a flaw, or a problem. Then I make a decision to exchange the tie. Now, I can't just go to the store and get a new one for free. I have to take in the old one. When I give up the flawed tie, I will receive a new tie. I exchange the old for the new. I now have a renewed tie.

Many people want to think God's thoughts, so they listen to preachers, read the Bible, read books, and listen to tapes. But they never get anywhere, because they will not give up their old way of thinking. They can't get the new until they give up the old. Their mind is not being renewed. Being a transformed Christian does not mean adding a few positive virtues to your old carnal mind. It means becoming a whole new person.

The thing you don't want to change in your head, the thought, or way of thinking you don't want to give up, is the very thing that will stop you from doing God's will. The one thing you are blocking in your mind, and don't want to change, or don't want to do anything about, is the one thing that will keep you from the perfect will of God.

I know of a man who completely lost the joy of his salvation, and completely lost the good life that God gave to him, because he would not give up cigarettes. "Do you mean cigarettes could send a man to hell?" No, but they could put you into hell on earth. Cigarettes were the one thing he didn't want to change, and pretty soon he started feeling guilty. Every time he came to church, he smelled like cigarette smoke. He got so uptight because of the way he smelled, he didn't want to come to church. Pretty soon, the only people he could hang around, were other people who smoked. The other people who smoked were drinking wine and beer. So eventually, he was having a beer with his cigarettes. Before he realized it, he was off into the whole life style. The last time I heard from him, he was calling from the county jail.

He was a good Christian. In fact, he was one of the people who influenced me to become a Christian. But because he refused to change that one thing, it drug him down, and he lost everything he had.

Some of you have been caught up in traditions. You are hung up by a tradition that doesn't mean anything to God. But it is so important to you, and you refuse to give it up.

That is one area the devil will use to tear you down.

Paul said, "Give no place to the devil". In the Greek, that says, 'Give no foothold to the devil'. The devil doesn't need much to grasp a hold of to drag you down. All he needs is a little foothold. If he can get one little toe in there, he'll wiggle it around, and keep working on it, and gnawing on it. Pretty soon he has his whole foot in there. When he gets his foot in, he'll get his hands in, and he'll start pulling, and prying on that thing until he has opened himself a wide door. He'll just walk right in, and destroy you. All because of that one little thing you don't want to change. That's why Paul said, 'Be transformed by the renewing of your mind, and *then* you'll prove the good, and acceptable, and perfect will of God.'

Doing the mature will of God is not based on your years in the church, it's based on the renewing of your mind. There are many "old babies" in the church, and there are many "young elders". The "old babies" think the same way now, that they did 40 years ago. The "young elders" are being transformed by the renewing of their minds. It will not happen instantly. It is a never ending process. You will never have the total knowledge God has. You will always be learning.

If you come across something in the Word of God that you realize you don't believe, change it right there. That's what renewing the mind is all about. Casting down what we thought was right, and replacing it with what God says is right. When we do that, we can accomplish the "good, and acceptable, and perfect will of God."

Let's read Romans 12:2 from the Kenneth Wuest translation of the Bible.

> Stop assuming an outward expression that does not come from within you, and is not representative of what you are in your inner being.

On the inside, we are new creatures in Christ. On the inside, we are the righteousness of God. Our spirit has been born again. We are children of God, joint heirs with Christ. On the inside, we are clean, and holy, and pure. God sees us without spot or wrinkle. But on the outside, our behavior might be bad. You might have bad attitudes. You might be lazy. You might be bitter, and hostile towards people. All those outward expressions, all that negativity, does not represent who you really are. So, the Lord tells us to stop assuming an outward expression that does not come from within you, and does not represent who you are in your inner being.

Many Christians, even though they are born again, filled with the Spirit, and pray in other tongues, still pattern their life after what the world is doing today. They think like every other worldly person thinks. They talk like every other worldly person talks. They have the same problems that every other worldly person has. They are patterned after, and conformed to today's world.

God said, 'Change your outward expression to one that comes from within you, and is representative of your inner being'. How do you do that? You desire to be holy. You desire to walk the straight and narrow, and to enter into the straight gate which leads to life. How do you live that way? By the renewing of your mind.

People walk around many times, feeling bad, condemned, and guilty, and they don't know what to do to change. They've had every spirit they could think of cast out of them, but they are still the same. They've been inner healed, outer healed, healed upside down, and right side up, but they are *still the same*. The reason they are still the same is, they are not renewing their minds. If you are not changing your outward expression to conform to the inner being, which is the Spirit of God, nothing will change.

As you renew your mind, you enter into His fulness. You enter into that good, acceptable, and perfect will of God. That's where there is "joy unspeakable, and full of glory". That's where every day is a day of joy, and a day of peace, and a day of power. That's where every day is a day of victory. The devil doesn't even bother coming down your block, because he's so tired of having your foot on his head! That's where you walk in the total abundance of God. And that's available to every believer.

12
YOU HAVE A SOVEREIGN WILL

One day I was studying from God's Word about how man was created in the image and likeness of God (Genesis 1:26). I knew that meant we are eternal spirit beings just like God is, but then the Holy Spirit let me know that wasn't all it meant. He reminded me that angels and demons are spirit beings, but the Bible doesn't say they are in the image and likeness of God. The thing that sets man apart from every other creature is our will. We are *sovereign* over our own lives, just like God is.

Sovereign means, 'independent of all else'. If I am a sovereign dictator, I rule just like I want to. I am not required to heed anyone else. If I am a sovereign ruler, I have total, and complete authority, and no one else can say anything about it. If I have a sovereign will, I choose for myself. I go where I want to go. I do what I want to do, and I think what I want to think. That's what it means to have a sovereign will! You may have been influenced, but you still make your own choices. No one is in control of your life except you.

God is not in control of our lives. If God *was* in control of our lives, we would simply be robots, or puppets down here, waiting for God to jerk our string. But that's not what's happening. We have a will! Deuteronomy 30:19 says,

> I call heaven and earth to record this day against you, that I have set before you life and death, blessing and cursing; *therefore choose life,* that both thou and thy seed may live.

God does not decide whether we are blessed or cursed, or whether we live or die... *we do!* The Bible said that our will is so powerful, that we can spend our eternity in hell, if we choose, and God won't stop us. If we want to follow Satan, and spend eternity with him, God will protect our right to do so. "I put before you life, and death", and Jesus said, "Men love death rather than life."

The most powerful tool that God has given you in the 'natural' realm, is your will. Listen carefully to how I said that. In the 'natural', in just human elements, your will is the most powerful tool that God has given to you. God says, "I have set before you life and death, blessing or cursing... you choose."

You need to realize that everything in life, everything in the natural realm, falls under one of those two categories: life or death. *Everything.* Is a blessing life, or death? Is cursing life, or death? Is sickness life, or death? Is health life, or death? Is prosperity life, or death? Is poverty life, or death? God has set before you life and death, and everything you do is involved with one of those two things. And, *you* make the choice.

It is amazing how God created us. God put us on earth, and He placed before us life and death, blessing and cursing. He said, "therefore choose". But we go around saying, "Lord, whatever you want, whatever you want". God doesn't even acknowledge that, because He said, "You choose. Whatever *you* want!" The reason so many of us Christians have never progressed in our Christianity, is because we are 'waiting on the Lord'. "Not my will but thine be done." The only time that prayer should be prayed, is if we are praying a prayer of dedication, consecration, or surrender to the Lord for a ministry, or a family. In our daily life, in the things we have going on in our life every day ... *we* choose.

That may sound strange to some of you, because you have been so programmed that anything you desire is evil. "If I want it, it must be bad." Didn't Jesus say, "Whatsoever things *you* desire, when *you* pray, believe that ye receive it and ye shall have it" (Mark 11:24)? He didn't say what God desires, He said, "What you desire". Psalm 37:4 says,

> Delight thyself in the Lord and He will give thee the desires of your heart.

God has placed a will within you. He has placed the ability to choose, and the ability to desire within you. That is a God given gift.

Now, it's up to you to use it properly. You can use it for life, or you can use it for death.

Look in Genesis 1:26,27. I want to show you something about the way we were created.

> And God said, Let us make man in our image, after our likeness: and let them have dominion over the fish of the sea, and over the fowl of the air, and over the cattle, and over all the earth, and over every creeping thing that creepeth upon the earth. So God created man in his own image, in the image of God created he him; male and female created he them.

In the Hebrew, that is literally translated, "God created man and woman an exact *duplicate* of Himself."

You are the closest thing to God that will ever be in existence. You are higher than angels, higher than cherubims, higher than seraphims, higher than any being, any animal, any creature, any thing that will ever be in existence. You are as close to God in likeness, as is possible. You are an exact duplicate in kind to the Heavenly Father. It is your sovereign will that makes you to be an exact duplicate.

When the tree of the knowledge of good and evil was placed in the garden of Eden, man had a choice. He could follow God, obey God, serve God, love God; or he could choose to rebel, choose to resist. He could choose to go another way, and serve another lord. God told him exactly what would happen if he would use his will. He told him, 'If you will serve me, you'll have dominion. Every need will be met. You'll have abundance. If you eat of the tree of good and evil, you will die'. The Hebrew says, "in dying thou shalt die". He meant you'll die spiritually now, and you'll die physically in some period of time. That was man's choice. The Bible said, Adam was fully aware of his choice. Eve was deceived. Eve didn't understand the circumstances, but Adam knew exactly what he was doing. He chose to reject the commandment of God, to reject the Word of God. He chose to commit high treason, and submit himself to the devil. That was *his* choice.

In every circumstance of life, you have God, and you have a tree of knowledge of good and evil, and you have an enemy. Every one of us faces that. We can do our own thing. Go with what we think. Go with what we know, and what we want to do, *or* we can go with God. It's totally up to us. It's totally our choice.

The devil can't make you do anything, and God can't make you do anything. In every area of life, in everything that you do, *you* have a choice. In every circumstance, every situation, you choose. Joshua 24:15 says,

> And if it seem evil unto you to serve the Lord, choose you this day whom ye will serve; whether the gods which your fathers served that were on the other side of the flood, or the gods of the Amor-

ites, in whose land ye dwell: but as for me and my house, we will serve the Lord.

Joshua made it so clear. If you want to serve other gods, go on and serve them. If you want to serve the god of your father, do it. Whatever, or whoever you want to serve, do it. He said, "As for me and my house, we *will* ..." Notice what he said, we *will.* It's an act of your will. It's your choice, your decision, your desire. It's what you want.

Every soul in heaven will be there because they chose it. And on the other side, every soul in hell, every person in hell, is there because they chose it. If you are in heaven on earth, it's because you chose it. If you are in hell on earth, it's because you chose it. Proverbs 1:25-29 is a key to the kingdom of God that will cause you to have a wonderful life. If you can grasp hold of this, it will set you free.

> But ye have set at nought all my counsel, and would none of my reproof; I also will laugh at your calamity; I will mock when your fear cometh; When your fear cometh as desolation, and your destruction cometh as a whirlwind; when distress and anguish cometh upon you. Then shall they call upon me, but I will not answer; they shall seek me early, but they shall not find me: For that they hated knowledge, and did not choose the fear of the Lord.

When you get to the point where everything has failed. Your money is gone, your health is gone, *and* your friends are gone. When you are so drunk that you can't drink anymore, or you can't get anymore loaded, and you cry out, "Oh God, help me!", He said, 'I'm going to laugh at your calamity, because you decided against my ways. You hated knowledge, and *you* choose what you did. You did not choose the fear of the Lord.' It always, always comes back to your choice.

Thank God for His mercy. Thank God that even when we choose the wrong thing, if we will truly repent, and ask His forgiveness, if we truly change, He will help us. *Because,* "His mercy endureth forever."

Everything is based around your will power. Why did God put Adam in the garden with the tree of the knowledge of good and evil, and say don't eat it? Because God gave man a choice. If God had given man a will, but nothing to use his will on, then man would have been nothing more than a puppet. God is not interested in having puppets. God already has a multitude of angels. He doesn't want, or need more angels. He wants beings who choose Him, who follow Him, because they love Him.

Sometimes people say to me, "Casey, how can I change all my thinking?" They are looking for one answer, in 25 words or less. Something they can do right now, so that everything will be different. But that's not where it's at. John 8:31-32 says,

> Then said Jesus to those Jews which
> believed on him, If ye continue in my
> word, then are ye my disciples indeed.

He said, 'If'. If speaks of a condition. Also, He didn't say, 'If you go to church every Sunday, you are my disciple'. He didn't say, 'If you have a Bible on your coffee table, you are my disciple'. He said, "If you continue in my Word". That means abiding in, continuing in, dwelling in, living in. It's a life style.

When people are taught on prosperity, or healing, or some other temporal benefit of being a Christian, they get caught up with it, and think, "Wow! I'm going to become a Christian so I can prosper, and have all of these wonderful, temporal benefits", and they want it *now*. Well, when everything doesn't change immediately, they think, "I knew this wasn't going to work. I knew it was too good to be real!" It *is* real, but it takes continuing in the Word of God, to be a disciple of Christ.

Your will, or your power to choose, given to you by the Father, is a force that you must use to renew your minds. God already knows the things you are going to do, but that doesn't change the fact that the choice is yours. You can choose life or death, blessing or cursing. The terrible thing about hell, is that men have already been forgiven, and the price for freedom is paid, but they choose to spend eternity separated from God. You choose who you will serve. Joshua said, 'As for my house, we *will* serve the Lord.' We *will*. Romans 10:9 says,

That if thou shalt confess with thy mouth the Lord Jesus, and shalt believe in thine heart that God raised him from the dead, thou shalt be saved.

Once again it said, "If". That signifies you have a choice to make. You don't have to get saved. You don't have to accept the Lord. You don't have to go to heaven. *It's up to you!*

Your will is the key in being spiritually minded. You must use your will, and make yourself be spiritually minded. At first you'll feel very weak because you've not exercised your will. You've just kind of gone with the flow. Whatever happened to come along, that's what you did. So your will becomes weak, indecisive, and unable to handle major decisions. You must exercise your will, and begin to build it up. Start out with small things like: I will pray 15 minutes every day. I will read the Word 15 minutes every day. Then keep on growing, and increasing your will power, by disciplining your life more, and more. It won't be long until major decisions will be simple, and you'll have control over your life.

You are responsible for your thoughts, decisions, actions, and words. That's why the Bible teaches that you will be judged for your deeds, and words, because you are in control of them. Whatever you do, and say, is up to your will.

I had a hard time believing this when I first became a Christian, because it seemed like some of the things I thought, or did I could not change. I felt like I couldn't help myself. They just happened because of some strange outside force. Often times people will say, "I tried but I couldn't help myself." I had to realize that for many years I had been training my mind to work in certain ways, and I had many unscriptural habits. It took hard, consistent work on my thinking, and behavior to get it changed, and following the Word of God. Don't be discouraged if you feel like the fight is long and hard. You didn't get where you are right now over night, and you won't change over night. The important thing is that you continue to use your will, and drive all negativity out of your life.

13
YOUR WILL IN LINE
WITH GOD'S WILL

Your will can be trained. You can train your will to only make positive decisions, and to reject all negativity. You can train your will to *only* agree with God's will. That's what Jesus was doing in the Garden of Gethsemane. He said, "Not my will but your will." He had to make a decision to do God's will. And *you* have to use *your* will to do God's will. If you do that, you will be a success. Remember, God is never going to come down here, put you in a headlock, and make you do anything.

Some ministers had gathered together to pray. Their prayer was, "Break us Lord, just break us. Make us feel bad Lord, so that we will go out and do what we know we are supposed to do. Oh, give us a burden, Lord. Keep us up all night with a burden for the people. Break us!" Now, that sounds very spiritual, but what they were really saying was, "Lord, we know what we are supposed to do, but we don't want to, so would you make us?" That's really what they were saying. Praise God, He's *not* breaking me!

Do you know what a broken person is? Useless. God does not want broken people. He wants people who are using *their will* to do His will. We've all seen parents who have broken the will of their children. They have pounded, and pounded on the children until those kids break. And after that, that child does nothing. They are depressed. They have no strength, no power, no drive. God doesn't want His children like that. God wants us motivated, powerful, strong, supernatural people. He *wants* us to do His will, and *we* have the power to do that.

In our society, and I suppose it is true in every culture, the natural tendency, is to have a scapegoat. Someone we can blame for the situation. Look at Luke 10:38-42.

> Now it came to pass, as they went, that he entered into a certain village: and a certain woman named Martha received him into her house. And she had a sister called Mary, which also sat at Jesus' feet, and heard his word. But Martha was cumbered about much serving, and came to him, and said, Lord, dost thou not care that my sister hath left me to serve alone? Bid her therefore that she help me. And Jesus answered and said unto her, Martha, Martha, thou art careful and troubled about many things: but one thing is needful: and Mary hath chose that good part, which shall not be taken away from her.

For the Christian, it is easy to say either God did it, or the devil did it. The Lord made this happen, and the devil made that happen. And, of course, we can always blame other people. "If it wasn't for my wife, I would be happy. If it wasn't for my kids, I'd be happy. If my parents would ever get straightened out, I could live a good life." Then, we have the police, or the boss, or the neighbors, or the dog, or the government, or the President, or the communists, or the Russians, and on, and on. There is always something that is causing us to be in the condition we are in.

When you talk to the average person, they will have several excuses why they are depressed, or why they are not succeeding, or why their business is not working right. You will never hear them saying, "Well, I am just doing what I want to do. I chose this." No one wants to say that. They want to put it on someone else. I would be happy if... I would be successful if... but it's their choice, their responsibility. They do what they want to do. If they don't like what they are doing now, they can do something else. They're in control.

If you don't like where you are, change it. "But Brother Treat, I don't know how." Find out how. "Well, I don't want to." There comes the truth. You like to gripe about what you're doing. You like to complain, and moan, and groan, and when it comes right down to it, that's what you want! If it wasn't what you wanted, you would change it.

It's a sad thing, but Pastors are some of the worst gripers you will ever find. "Oh Brother Treat, I'm under such a burden. You know how it is in the ministry." Yeah, it's a blast! People are so much fun to help. I love to be with people! "Oh, but they're a heavy load." No, they're a joy! See, you can do it however *you* want to do it. If you don't like it, change it. That's all there is to it.

So many times you'll hear people say, "I really like to pray, but I just can't. I don't have time. I don't know how." That's a lie! You pray when you want to pray. If you don't want to pray, you don't pray. If someone asks you, "Do you pray?", just say, "No", if that's the truth. "How come?" "Because I don't want to." Don't tell them you don't have time. Don't tell them the kids keep you busy. Don't tell them about your job, and your house, and all those other excuses. You don't pray, because *you don't want to.*

If you can't change something you don't like, or you don't want to change something you don't like, then learn to like it. "Do you mean that I can like getting up, and going to work?" Sure you can. It's a blast. You can like it. "Do you mean I can like having to do my responsibilities?" Sure, who told you responsibilities were negative? I like mine. I enjoy them. You'll find me feeling good at any time of the day. Sometimes people get mad at me, because they think I shouldn't, or can't feel good all the time. Yes I can, because I enjoy what I am doing.

You have a will, and you can develop your will to be positive, or to be negative. You can choose to be irresponsible, lazy, miserable, depressed, and some of you do. That's just the way you want to be. *Or,* you can choose to be happy, free, full of vim, vigor, and vitality. You make the choice. God has given you the power to choose. From the day He breathed the breath of life into Adam, and Adam became a living soul, that soul has been making choices.

So many of you have been taught that the Lord is in control, and God chooses how you will live. God just chooses to bless some folks, and curse other folks. God chooses for some to be happy, and some to be sad; for some to be rich, and some to be poor; for some to be strong, and some to be weak. You just have to hope that you get in the right line when He's handing out your future. If you happen to get in the wrong line, and get the wrong thing from God; no matter what you do, you're going to be cursed. No matter how you try, you're going to be miserable. No matter where you go, you're going to fail. That's the way a lot of people think.

I was trained, as a teenager, that many things were just left up to 'fate'. That means, you don't have any choice. There were these little clouds called 'fate' floating around in the universe, and there was a good one, and there was a bad one. If the good cloud happened to get on you, well look out, you were going to have a good time. But if the bad cloud happened to float by your house, you were going to be miserable, and everything you did would fail. I believed that it must be true, because it was obvious that some people were making it, and some were not. But that's a lie. That's wrong. That's not the truth. The Bible teaches that, "God has set before us life and death, blessing and cursing, therefore choose."

Look at Luke 5:3-5. Jesus was teaching by the Sea of Galilee, and He saw two ships standing by the lake. The fishermen left their ships, and were washing their nets.

> And he entered into one of the ships, which was Simon's and prayed him that he would thrust out a little from the land. And he sat down, and taught the people out of the ship. Now when he had left speaking, he said unto Simon, Launch out into the deep, and let down your nets for a draught.

Now remember, Jesus was a carpenter, and teacher, and He was telling a fisherman how to fish.

> And Simon answering said unto him, Master, we have toiled all night, and have taken nothing.

Think about this for a minute. Here's a fisherman. He's a professional in his field, and he does this for a living. His partners are fishermen, and every day, or every night, they are out fishing. Now here comes a preacher, and He starts telling them what to do. He's telling the fishermen to launch out into the deep, and let down their nets for a big bunch of fish. Simon said, 'Master, we've toiled all night. We've been fishing all night long, and we've taken nothing. We've already tried everything.' Listen to what Simon goes on to say,

At thy word, *I will.*

He said, "Nevertheless, at your word, I will." There is a choice in everything you will face in your life. When you feel like sinning, like telling a lie, like sliding something under the table, like cheating a little on your income tax; you are faced with that choice. You can say, "Lord, you said, be thou holy, even as you were holy. Even though I don't feel like it, *at thy word I will.*" When you feel like giving up, throwing up your hands, and saying, "This stuff doesn't work! I'm a failure. I'm never going to get healed. I am never going to get my bills paid. I am never going to get my family straightened out", you can say, "Lord, at your Word, I will believe." Everything you do is based on choice.

When you say, "I don't believe in that prayer stuff. I don't believe in that talking in tongues business. I'm not going for this healing and prosperity. I know God made me sick, and bless God, I'm going to stay sick." What you are saying is, "Nevertheless Lord, at your Word, *I won't!*" That's what you say, because the Bible said, 'Believe and you will be healed'. The Bible said, 'All your needs are met according to His riches in glory'. It's your choice. You are responsible for your world. If you don't like the way you are living, you can change it. Remember, you decide whether you live positive, or negative. You choose to train your will to *agree* with God's will, or *not to agree* with God's will. *You choose.*

14
GOING AND GROWING

G od gave the ministry gifts, which are listed in Ephesians, to the body of Christ for a specific reason. So that we would grow. Ephesians 4:11,12 tells us,

> And he gave some, apostles; and some, prophets; and some, evangelists; and some, pastors and teachers; For the perfecting of the saints, for the work of the ministry, for the edifying of the body of Christ.

Why did God give us the ministry gifts? For the *perfecting* of the saints, or for the *maturing* of the saints, or for the *growing up* of the saints. He did not give them for the entertaining, for the satisfying, or for the comforting of the saints. Go on to verse 13.

> Till we all come in the unity of the faith, and of the knowledge of the Son of God, unto a perfect man, unto the measure of the stature of the fulness of Christ.

We're all supposed to be growing until we come into unity of the faith, and until we are mature men and women. Until we reach the fullness of Christ. That means, we have to keep on changing, and growing, and renewing our minds because we have a long way to go. Verses 14 & 15.

> That we henceforth be no more children, tossed to and fro, and carried about with every wind of doctrine, by the sleight of men, and cunning craftiness, whereby they lie in wait to deceive; But speaking the truth in love, may grow up into him in all things, which is the head, even Christ.

That we may grow up into Him, in all things. Our goal is to grow up into Him. We're not just to be comfortable. Not just to be satisfied. Not just to be content. We want to grow up into Jesus. That means, be more like Him. Look at Mark 4:30-32.

> And he said, 'Whereunto shall we liken the kingdom of God? or with what comparison shall we compare it? It is like a grain of mustard seed, which, when it is sown in the earth, is less than all the seeds that be in the earth: But when it is sown, it groweth up, and becometh greater than all herbs, and shooteth out great branches; so that the fowls of the air may lodge under the shadow of it.

The whole kingdom of God is like a seed. It grows up. When the seed is planted, it starts out very small, and becomes very large. It becomes greater. If you are part of the kingdom of God, then you must be growing.

Do you know that God wants you to become greater tomorrow than you are today. He wants you to be a greater wife. You're good now, but He wants you to become greater. He wants you to be a greater business woman, a greater minister, a greater teacher. "It groweth up, and becometh greater!" God wants you to grow so you'll be greater. Ephesians 4:17-24 says,

> This I say therefore, and testify in the Lord, that ye henceforth walk not as other Gentiles walk in the vanity of their mind. Having the understanding darkened, being alienated from the life of God through the ignorance that is in them, because of the blindness of their heart. Who being past feeling have given themselves over unto lasciviousness, to work all uncleanness with greediness. But ye have not so learned Christ. If so be that ye have heard him, and have been taught by him, as the truth is in Jesus. That ye put off concerning the former conversation the old man, which is corrupt according to the deceitful lusts; And be renewed in the spirit of your mind. And that ye put on the new man, which after God is created in righteousness and true holiness.

He says, 'take off the old man, don't be conformed to this world'. Take off those old habits, that old way of thinking, that old way of acting, those old attitudes, and behaviors. Take them off. Be renewed in the spirit of your mind.

Have you ever heard someone say, "Well, he's in good spirits today." That means, he has a good attitude today. He said, "Be renewed in the attitude of your mind! Take off that old man, and put on the new man, which after God, is created in righteousness, and true holiness."

Start living a righteous, holy life. How? Be renewed in the attitude of your mind. Change the way you think. Start thinking differently. This gift of God, to be able to change the way we think, is the most powerful thing God gave to you, other than being born again, and filled with the Holy Ghost. Because it is the key to enjoying the life of righteousness, and true holiness.

Learning is not enough. Learning is just gaining knowledge, gaining information, just storing it up. Memorizing verses, hearing sermons, reading books, going to church, pouring it all in, is not the answer. That won't change you. That won't make you grow up in the Lord. When you take off the old man, the old way of thinking, it's not there anymore. You don't have any problem with it. Paul said, "I'm dead to the world." When you are dead to the world, the world can't influence you, but if you haven't taken off the old man, it still can. It can get back in there, and mess you up.

Unless you take that old man off, he'll keep sneaking through. He will keep popping up. And you'll find yourself with the same old troubles, same old problems, same old circumstances. You say, "I don't understand it. I know everything everyone in the world ever preached. In fact, I could preach better than most of them, but I'm still struggling. I'm still bumping along." Why? Because the old man is still hanging on. Even though you have covered it up really pretty, you still have the same old man underneath.

Renewing the mind, and growing, and changing requires you to be able to say, "I was wrong. I made the wrong decision, I did the wrong thing." If you cannot do that, you will never grow. Sin can never be erased until it is confessed. 'Confess your sins, and He is faithful, and just to cleanse you, and forgive you'. (I John 1:9) You have to confess it first.

I've had to come into services, and say, "I was wrong. I used to think this, but I was wrong." I've had to say it more than I wanted to, but if I want to keep on growing, I'm going to have to continue to do that. I have to be willing to say, "I was wrong."

When you say "I was wrong", God can put new knowledge into you. You can put on the new man, and be renewed in the spirit of your mind. You can start doing something different, and it will work. Some of you have this prideful attitude, "Bless God, don't tell me I'm wrong.

I'm the righteousness of God. I'm a new creature in Christ. I can do all things through Christ. Don't you dare confront me with any of that kind of stuff." I know you're righteous, and I know you're a new creature. I know you are on your way to heaven, but that doesn't mean all of your thinking is right. Look at Colossians 3:1,2.

> If ye then be risen with Christ, seek those things which are above, where Christ sitteth on the right hand of God. Set your affection on things above, not on things on the earth.

What are your affections? The Greek text literally means, 'your thoughts'. Set your thoughts, or your mind, or your thinking on things above. What you do with your head decides how you are going to live your Christian life. Verses 3-5

> For ye are dead, and your life is hid with Christ in God. When Christ, who is our life, shall appear, then shall ye also appear with him in glory. Mortify therefore your members which are upon the earth.

Why did he say 'you are dead' in one verse, and then turn right around and say, 'put those negative things to death' in another verse? Because, spiritually speaking, you are already dead, and hid in Christ Jesus. But physically speaking, you have to take authority over your members that are on the earth. Take authority over your flesh. Those things are going to rise up if you don't renew your mind. Go to verse 8.

> But now ye also put off all these: anger, wrath, malice, blasphemy, filthy communication out of your mouth. Lie not one to another, seeing that ye have put off the old man with his deeds. And have put on the new man, which is renewed in knowledge after the image of him that created him.

Put off the old man, put on the new man, which is renewed in knowledge. You can't put the new man on until you take the old man off. When you put off that old man, that old behavior, that old attitude, that old way of thinking, and replace it with a new way in line with the Word of God, and the will of God; then you can begin to enjoy your Christian life.

You don't have to be the same for 40 years. Don't stay in a rut. Move on. Be better, be greater. Receive all that God has for you. He's given you that ability. It comes when you will admit, "I'm wrong! I'm going to get something new." Put on the new man, and go on with God.

God predestinated, preplanned, preordained that you should be changed, molded, and conformed, to the image of Jesus. Romans 8:29 says,

For whom he did foreknow, he also did predestinate to be conformed to the image of his Son, that he might be the firstborn among many brethren.

To change, or to grow in the Lord, means that every day we are being more like Jesus. More and more, we think the way He thinks. More and more, we act the way He acts. More and more, we walk like He walked. That's what changing is all about. Being like Jesus!

You need to ask yourself, "Am I doing, right now, what Jesus would do?" If you say, "No, He wouldn't act this way", then you need to take off the old man, put on the new man, and act like Jesus. If you're scared, and nervous, and shook up, then you need to say, "Wait a minute! Is this the way Jesus was?" When they came to Him with a problem, did He say, "Oh no, get my valiums!" No! Take that old man off. Say, "I don't need pills, I don't need tranquilizers. I take off that old man. I put off fear. I put off worry. I put off anxiety. I cast my care on you Lord." Put on the new man full of faith. Proverbs 3:5,6 says,

Trust in the Lord with all your heart, and lean not to your own understanding. In all your ways acknowledge Him.

Get rid of the old man, and conform to the image of Jesus.

The Christian life is not a struggle. It is not

hard. Jesus' yoke is not hard, His burden is not heavy. He said, "My burden is light, my yoke is easy". Be renewed in the spirit of your mind, and put on the new man.

15
THE ULTIMATE GOAL

We know that God has provided an abundant life for all of us. He has provided a way for us to receive that abundant life, and walk in the blessings of God. It is by the renewing of our minds. Praise God, we can virtually live in heaven on earth. But why? Why would God want us to grow, and change, and become more like Jesus here on earth? He could just take us to heaven when we get born again, and we could instantly have all those things.

There is one more aspect of growing, and changing, and renewing of the mind that I want to show you, and make very clear to you. Look again at Ephesians 4:11-15.

> And he gave some, apostles; and some prophets; and some, evangelists; and some pastors and teachers; for the perfecting of the saints for the work of the ministry, for the edifying of the body of Christ: Till we all come in the unity of the faith, and of the knowledge of the Son of God, unto a perfect man, unto the measure of the stature of the fullness of Christ: That we hence forth be no more children, tossed to and fro, and carried about with every wind of doctrine, by

the sleight of men, and cunning craftiness, whereby they lie in wait to deceive; But speaking the truth in love, may grow up into him in all things, which is the head, even Christ.

Jesus gave to the ministry apostles, prophets, evangelists, and teachers, so that the church, and the saints would be mature, or would be perfected, or *grow up.* But notice what verse 12 says, "For the perfecting of the saints for the work of the ministry". What the Bible is saying, is the leadership of the church is to be perfecting the church, so that *they* will do the work of the ministry.

In the past, there has come about a way of thinking, that has separated the clergy from the laymen. It separated the ministers from the church members. The way many people believed, and there are some who still do, is that the clergy: the pastors, the priests, the teachers of the church, were there to do the work of the ministry. The church members, or the congregation were there just to sit and listen. At one point, it got to the place where people couldn't even have their own Bibles. They couldn't read the Bible on their own, because it was against their religious practices. It was sinful for the common church member to own a Bible.

Today that tradition, that bondage, for the most part, has been broken. The devil brought that into being to get the Word out of people, to keep it away from the people. Now people have their own Bibles. People are now realizing that they are a part of the church. They are workers together with the Lord. Yet many still have the mentality that, the "pastor" does the work of the church, and everyone else is *just* the congregation. That is wrong, that is negative, and that's not the truth. The church body has just as much responsibility to do the work of the ministry as the pastor does. The only difference is, the pastor has the responsibility to teach the people, so that they can do more work in the ministry, and do it better.

This is one reason why I don't want people calling me Reverend, or Pastor Treat. Those names aren't bad, but it gives people the mentality that I am different. There is no difference. We are both responsible for the work of the ministry.

This is how verse 12 reads in the Amplified Bible.

> His intention was the perfecting and full equipping of the saints. That they should do the work of ministering toward building up Christ's body, the church.

The pastor is supposed to be equipping the people with knowledge, with faith, with understanding, with wisdom, with strength, to do the work of the ministry.

When you think about it, there is no way the pastor can do *all* the work of the ministry. It's impossible. But he can equip you, and you can do the work of the ministry. When you are renewing your mind, and changing in God, then you will be increasing in your work of the ministry. You'll be doing things with the Lord, and for people. You'll be increasing what you're doing to help others.

The Word tells us that we are to be teaching all nations about Jesus. Matthew 28:19, 20 says,

> Go ye therefore, and teach all nations, baptizing them in the name of the Father, and of the Son, and of the Holy Ghost: Teaching them to observe all things whatsoever I have commanded you: and, lo, I am with you alway, even unto the end of the world.

He did not say, 'go get people born again'. He did not say, 'go and hand out tracts'. He did not say, 'go out with a sign that says repent'. He said, "Go and teach all nations". In the Greek that literally means, "Go, and make disciples". A disciple is a disciplined one who goes, and follows the Lord. A disciple of Jesus, is one who has disciplined himself to follow Jesus.

Where so many Christians have missed it, and have been discouraged, is in thinking that when you get born again, that's the end. There is no more until you get to heaven. That's not what Christianity is all about. When you get born again, you have just joined the ranks. You've just become a soldier. You said, "Yes, I'll take up my weapons. Yes, I'll go to war against the devil, and against all the evil in this world. Yes, I'll be a soldier in the army of the Lord." You didn't say, "Yes, I'll sit back and rest til I get to heaven." You said, "Yes, I'll be a disciple."

We need to realize that Christianity is renewing our minds, exchanging our thinking for God's thinking, and growing up to be more like Jesus every day. What did Jesus do with all of His life, with all of His strength? He helped people. A Christian is a person who is changing, and growing every day, so that he can continually do more to help others. A Christian is not a selfish one. A Christian is not just interested in what he can *get*, but he is interested in what he can *do* for someone else. Disciples are people who follow the Lord. Disciples are not people who say 'Jesus' one time, and then go about their business. II Corinthians 4:16 says,

> For which cause we faint not; but though our outward man perish, yet the inward man is renewed day by day.

If you are involved with the Lord, involved with the Holy Spirit, involved with the Bible, you are being renewed day by day. You are becoming different. You are growing. You are going. You are changing. And you are interested in helping people to receive the life of God. Like Jesus, you give your life to meet the needs of others.

16
THE RESULTS OF RENEWING THE MIND

If you are being renewed day by day, then every day is exciting. Every day something good is going to happen. You're looking forward to it. You're reaching for it. You are expectant about what God might do in your life today.

When you change, and grow, four things happen.

1) *You think differently.* Your mind is not occupied with the same thoughts. You don't think about the things that you used to think about. You don't like the things that you used to like. Your mind is filled with a completely new way of thinking. You don't have the same mentality that you used to.

2) *You feel different.* Although you don't live by feelings when you are growing, you *do* feel different. You have more life in you, more freedom, more joy, more liberty. Growing is a feeling. There's a motivation, an excitement, a challenge that feels good on the inside of you. You're going, you're moving, and you're feeling good about it. When you change, you feel different.

3) *You act different.* People start saying, "What's different about you? You're not the

same person you used to be." You're a different person. You're being renewed, you're changing, and growing in God, therefore, you act different.

4) *You receive different.* When you start growing, you start receiving blessings. You grow up to receive the things of God. When I was out in the world, I only received bad things. Every day I received something bad: flat tire, car would break down, pulled over by the police. Every day something bad would happen. But when I became a Christian and I started renewing my mind, it seemed like all those bad things stopped happening to me. Now, I only receive good things. I have people come to me, and give me hugs, and shake my hand. People bless me, and help me, and love me. Those are the only things I receive. When you change, you begin to receive different.

Growth is the key to God's abundant blessings. When you are born again, you don't automatically receive all the abundant blessings of salvation. There are a lot of things about being a Christian that you are not enjoying yet. A lot of people are born again, and don't know about the peace of God. A lot of people, are born again, but they don't have the joy of the Lord. The reason is that renewing the mind, changing, growing up, are the keys to His abundant blessings. II Peter 3:18 says,

> But grow in grace, and in the knowledge of our Lord, and Saviour Jesus Christ.

Grace is God's will, or willingness to use His power on our behalf, even though we don't deserve it. Grace is God's willingness to bless you, even though you don't deserve it. Grow in grace. Grow in your 'reception', or in your 'acceptance' of God's willingness to bless you.

When you first have a baby, that baby is as human as he will ever be. He's as much a person, as any person can be. But, he cannot enjoy most things in this life. He can't enjoy T-bone steak, he has to eat baby food. Have you noticed in the grocery store, that every bottle of baby food looks exactly the same, MUSH! He can't enjoy the things that you, and I, as adults enjoy. He can't enjoy skiing down a mountain. He's too little. There are a lot of things you won't, and can't give him because he's too small.

It's the same way with young Christians. They never receive certain things from God, because they are too young to receive it, or too young to use it properly. But renewing their minds and changing will enable them to receive the abundant blessings God has to offer. The more they grow in the Lord, the more they can receive of God's blessings, and the more fun their Christian life will be. No matter what their age, growing and changing is the key to walking in God's blessing. Look at Mark 4:26.

> And he said, So is the kingdom of God, as if a man should cast seed into the ground; and should sleep, and rise night

and day, and the seed should spring and grow up, he knoweth not how. For the earth bringeth forth fruit of herself; first the blade, then the ear, after that the full corn in the ear, but when the fruit is brought forth, immediately he putteth in the sickle, because the harvest is come.

The whole kingdom of God operates as a seed. It has to grow before you can reap the fruit. In this chapter, Jesus started out with the parable of the sower, who sowed the Word. The seed is the Word of God. Where was the seed sown in the parable? The natural seed is sown in the ground, or in the earth. The spiritual seed He was talking about, is sown in the human heart. The seed of the Word of God, is sown in your heart, and groweth up, and produces fruit. Read the parable in verse 26 in that way.

So is the kingdom of God, as if a man should cast seed into his *heart.* And should sleep, and rise night and day.

In other words, go about his business. Let's continue.

And the seed should spring and grow up, he knoweth not how. For the *heart* bringeth forth fruit of itself, first the blade then the ear, after that the full corn in the ear. But when the fruit is

brought forth, immediately he putteth
in the sickle, because the harvest is
come.

The fruit of your life, the blessings of your
life, are going to come out of your heart. And
you have to be growing to provide opportunity
for your harvest to grow. Matthew 12:35 says,

A good man out of the good treasure of
the heart bringeth forth good things:
and an evil man out of the evil treasure
bringeth forth evil things.

If you have not been receiving what you want,
start renewing your mind, and growing. Begin
to progress in your Christian life, and then you
will leave room for the seed in your heart to
grow. Then you'll bring forth good things.
Good things do not fall on people out of the sky.
People bring them forth, and the way you
bring them forth is by growing. You grow by
renewing your mind, changing the way you
think, making God's thoughts your thoughts.

You will never enjoy the blessings, the
riches, and the fullness of Christianity, *unless*
you are pursuing, and actively renewing your
mind to the Word of God. That's when things
are good. That's when life is fun. The more you
grow, the better it gets.

I want to give you five evidences of Christian
growth or maturity. These five virtues from
the Word of God are signs, or evidence that you
are a mature Christian.

1) *Commitment.* A mature person knows how to, and regularly, makes commitments. An immature person cannot make a commitment. A commitment is when you do what you have said, and you do not back out of obligations. If you said it, you do it. You are sold out, 100% in, even though you may not feel like doing it. A person who makes commitments is trustworthy, and faithful. Commitment is a sign of maturity. Look at Psalm 15:4.

> In whose eyes a vile person is condemned; but he honoreth them that fear the Lord. He that sweareth to his own hurt, and changeth not.

Sweareth to his own hurt, and changeth not. It didn't say you do what is comfortable. It said, when you say it, you do it whether you like it or not. You do it, even if it hurts. A committed person is a mature person.

2) *Discipline.* Luke 14:27

> And whosoever doth not bear his cross, and come after me, cannot be my disciple.

Disciple means 'disciplined'. A disciplined one, is one who has a strict, rigid, life style of obeying the Word of God. They are disciplined in their prayer life. They pray every day. They are disciplined in their physical health. If they have too much weight on their body, they get it off. Whatever they have to do, they take care of it. They are disciplined in the way they look. They look sharp. Be disciplined, that's Christian virtue.

3) *Holiness.* I Peter 1:15-16

> But as he which hath called you is holy, so be you holy in all manner of conversation.

Conversation means life style. Be holy in all manner of your life style. Every part of your life must be holy.

> Because it is written, Be ye holy, for I am holy.

If you want to hang around a holy God, you have to be a holy person. Hebrew 12:14 says,

> Follow peace with all men, and holiness, without which no man shall see the Lord.

Holiness means, to be pure and separate from all sin. Not conformed to the world. God wants you to be holy, pure, separate from sin, and different from the world. A mature Christian is a holy Christian. Holy people separate themselves from all the world, and negative things.

4) *Generosity.* A mature Christian is generous. He's a cheerful giver, a liberal giver. In Proverbs 11:25 it says,

> The liberal soul shall be made fat; and
> he that watereth shall be watered also
> himself.

Are you a liberal soul, or do you just give what you have to get by? You know, pay your tithe down to the penny or not even give a tenth of your income. When you go out to eat, you make sure that you don't have to pay for anybody else. Are you stingy, or are you liberal? A mature Christian is a generous, liberal giver. You enjoy giving. You just like to do it. You want to share. You don't concern yourself with every little detail, you just want to help others. That's a mature Christian.

5) *Loyalty.* A mature Christian is loyal. Loyalty means to be submitted, and committed to leadership. It means you will stand together in every situation. Romans 16:17

> Now I beseech you, brethren, mark
> them which cause divisions and
> offences contrary to the doctrine which
> ye have learned; and avoid them.

In II Thessalonians 3, Paul says, 'Pray for me that I might be spared from men that are in disharmony', people who are always causing strife. Pray that I get away from these people. A mature Christian doesn't talk bad when things are going bad. A mature Christian doesn't talk bad about other people, even when they do something bad. He's loyal.

Be committed. Be disciplined. Be holy. Be generous. Be loyal. That's the best way to live. And that's where you get involved with the riches of God's abundance. Ephesians 4:15,16

> But speaking the truth in love, may grow up into him in all things, which is the head, even Christ. From whom the whole body fitly joined together and compacted by that which every joint supplieth, according to the effectual working in the measure of every part, maketh increase of the body unto the edifying of itself in love.

You need to meditate on this. Paul uses the physical body as an example of the body of Christ. Jesus is the head. We are His body. Just like you have a head on your physical body. The whole church is joined together, fitted together, and compacted. That means, knit together like a piece of material. "By that which every joint supplieth." In other words, everyone is responsible, or has a part to play in joining the church together. Everyone of us has a part in causing the church to be strong, to fit together, and to work together. *Everyone of us.* Immature Christians say, "Our pastor did this, our pastor did that, our leader did this, and did that". But mature, or grown up Christians say, "What can I do? What is my part? I can help put this thing together. I can help grow together in the Lord. I can help this church to be stronger." If every Christian had that attitude, the church would be strong. Instead of splitting people up, we're bringing them together. We're helping them to get anchored. We're helping them to get solid. We're fitting and knitting the body together. Every person has a part to play in the process.

> According to the effectual working in the measure of every part, maketh increase of the body unto the edifying of itself in love.

We don't wait for God to drop Christians out of the sky. We don't hire a consulting firm to go out, and get more people to come into the church. The *church* edifies, increases, builds itself up. Pastors don't build up churches, *churches* build up churches. Elders don't increase churches, every person in the church increases the church. We all work to bring more people in, and to edify the church. That's every person's responsibility. "Maketh increase of itself."

You are a preacher if you are a Christian. You have the power of the Holy Ghost to be a witness, to be a preacher, and to build up the body of Christ. It happens by just giving what you have. Romans 1:16 says,

> For I am not ashamed of the gospel of Christ: for it is the power of God unto salvation to every one that believeth; to the Jew first, and also to the Greek.

I am not ashamed of Jesus. I am not ashamed that I am a new creature in Christ. I am not ashamed that I have new life. I am not ashamed that I have received the Holy Ghost, and talk in new tongues. I want to let everyone know about it. Some Christians are ashamed of the gospel, but Paul said, "I am not ashamed of the gospel. It is the power of God".

If you will say what the gospel says, it has the power to do the work. If you will tell others about Jesus, tell them what you have experienced, tell them what you have; the power will go to work. You don't have to be a pastor for the power to go to work. It will work for *you*. Be ready at all times to share the gospel. Don't be ashamed of it. Give it away. It's the power that will help other people. The gospel has the power, all you have to do is put it out there for people to receive it.

Casey Treat is best known for his uncompromising and straight forward teaching of God's Word.

Casey accepted the call of God at the age of 20. He had been living in what he thought was the "fast lane". After he accepted Jesus Christ as his Lord, he realized that his "fast lane" was in reality the slow lane to self destruction. He now has a strong desire to present God's Word in a challenging, life changing way. He believes, "If someone is not helped by it, it is a waste of time."

Casey pastors Christian Faith Center, in Seattle, Washington. He and his wife Wendy started the church in January 1980 with a group of 30 people. Others responded to the straight forward message that God's Word works, and now thousands of people attend weekly services.

In September 1983 Christian Faith Center dedicated a new 58,000 square foot building with a sanctuary seating more than 3,000 people. With the new space the ministry also opened an elementary school in addition to pre-school and day care.

Casey is the Founder of the Christian Faith Ministry Training Center which trains men and women to minister in the area to which

God has called them. He is also the Northwest Regional Director for the International Convention of Faith Churches and Ministers (ICFCM).

Casey's daily television and radio programs called The Word of Life with Casey Treat are helping thousands of people learn the powerful truths found in God's Word. Requests for the programs have come from across the United States, Canada, Mexico, and the Philippines where Casey and Wendy have ministered to hundreds of pastors. The television program is now seen in several cities around the United States. There is also a world wide distribution of Casey's books and teaching tapes covering many subjects.

Jesus said, "I am come that you may have life, and life more abundantly." Through Casey Treat Ministries people all over the world are learning that through faith in God's Word they can reap the benefits of a joyful, prosperous, healthy life God wants them to have.

HAVE YOU BEEN BORN AGAIN?

The first step to a successful Christian Life is that you be born again. The Bible says in John 3:3 "...Except a man be born again, he cannot see the kingdom of God." Every person *must* be born again to know God and have everlasting life.

Being born again is making a commitment. It is making Jesus the Lord of your life, your master, teacher, and guide. To change from your ways, to follow Jesus (Romans 10: 9-10).

Just say this simple prayer: God, I come to you in the name of Jesus. I ask you to come into my life. I confess with my mouth Jesus is my Lord, and I believe in my heart you raised Him from the dead. I thank you I am saved. Amen.

You are now born again! You are forgiven of your sins, and on your way to heaven. This is just the beginning of a new life. The Bible tells us in Romans 12:2 to renew our minds, "And be not conformed to this world, but be ye transformed by the renewing of your mind, that ye may prove what is that good, and acceptable and perfect will of God".

Send for my book "Living the New Life". This book will help you understand more about the new life you have chosen. Let me hear from you!

132

IS THERE A SPECIAL NEED IN YOUR LIFE? DO YOU NEED PRAYER? CASEY TREAT MINISTRIES HAS AN INTERCESSORY PRAYER TEAM, AND WE WILL PRAY FOR YOU. PLEASE LET US KNOW YOUR NEED, WHATEVER IT MAY BE, AND SEND IT TO:

Casey Treat Ministries
P.O. Box 98581
Seattle, Washington 98188
206 824-8188

OTHER BOOKS AND BOOKLETS BY CASEY TREAT

Prayer: What To Do Between Believing and Receiving

God's Financial Program

How to Receive the Baptism with the Holy Spirit

Living the New Life

Hindrances to Receiving Your Healing

Power of the Soul

Christian Foundations: The First Steps to Success

The Key to Successful Christian Living

God's Word for Every Circumstance

Leadership: God's Plan for Your Success

For a complete catalog of books and tape series by Casey Treat, or to receive Casey's quarterly publication write to:

Casey Treat
P.O. Box 98581
Seattle, Washington 98188